The Rutledge Book of
FOOTBALL

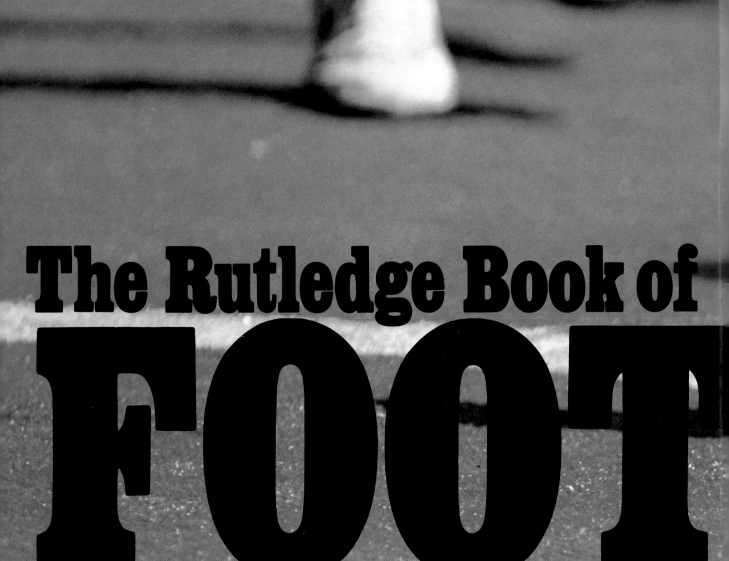

The Rutledge Book of
FOOT

Mike Rathet

The Rutledge Press
New York, New York

BALL

Acknowledgment

No amount of thanks can ever repay Joe Browne and Peter Abitante of the NFL for their assistance in this project and their patience with the author.

Edited by Deborah Weiss
Designed by Allan Mogel

Published by The Rutledge Press
A Division of W.H. Smith Publishers Inc.
112 Madison Avenue, New York, New York 10016

First printing 1981
Printed in Hong Kong

ISBN 0-8317-7597-1

Library of Congress Cataloging in Publication Data
Rathet, Mike.
 The Rutledge book of football
 1. Football—History.   2. National Football League—
History.   I. Title.
GV950.R37   796.332'09   81–5228
                            AACR2

Contents

1

George and Pete

"It's almost as though someone constructed the game of football knowing that fifty years later television would come along."
      Val Pinchbeck, NFL director of broadcasting

The year was 1919 and George Halas didn't know anything about television or, as it turned out, enough about hitting a curve ball. A former-University of Illinois star, Halas had been given the opportunity to join the New York Yankees for spring training that season, but the curve ball proved his undoing, and the club's right-field job went to a guy named Babe Ruth.

Having struck out in his bid for a major league baseball career, Halas went to work for the Chicago, Burlington and Quincy Railroad as a structural engineer calculating the stress and strain on new bridges. It wasn't exactly the kind of career the athletic Halas had envisioned, leaving him susceptible to the pleas of one A. E. Staley, who journeyed to Chicago from Decatur, Illinois, to convince Halas he was the man for a project he had in mind. Halas didn't know it, but he was about to trade railroad bridges for corn starch.

Staley, owner of a corn products company, promised Halas there would be less stress and strain on him if he came to Decatur and coached Staley's company football team. And he underscored his point by waving dollar bills at young George.

Money talked then just as it does now—although the sums being passed around are vastly different—and Halas succumbed to the blandishments offered by Staley when the numbers were put on the table. "He indicated he would be willing to pay me one hundred dollars a game, which I thought was a pretty good deal," Halas recalled. "It was over twice as much as I was making working all week for the Burlington."

Railroading's loss wasn't exactly corn starch's gain, but Halas was on his way to becoming as important to the growth of professional football as the Sultan of Swat was to major league baseball.

Halas—young, vibrant, imaginative, with a businessman's respect for a hard-earned dollar—took the knowledge he had gained as a player at Illinois and began to organize a group of men who would make corn starch during the week and play for the greater glory of the product on Sunday.

There wasn't much in it other than glory. The Staley-Halas union occurred while professional football was in its infant stage, company teams and town teams getting together on short notice, agreeing to rules and then playing on an open field. "Paid football was pretty much of a catch-as-catch-can affair in those days," Halas recalled in his autobiography. "Teams appeared one week and disappeared the next. Players came and went, drawn by the pleasure of playing. If others came to watch, that was fine. If they bought tickets, or tossed coins into a helmet passed by the most popular players, that was helpful."

The need was obvious—the sport had to have organization—and the result was a meeting on September 17, 1920, in the showroom of the automobile agency owned by Ralph Hays, who also managed the Canton (Ohio) Bulldogs. The showroom, stocked with Hupmobiles and Jordans, occupied the ground floor of the three-story Odd Fellows building. Twelve teams were represented, but not every one found a seat. "Chairs were few," Halas recalled. "I sat on a running board."

It didn't take long for the assembled to agree to the formation of the American Professional Football Association with the legendary Jim Thorpe as president and a $100 fee for membership. But the original members got away without paying a cent. "I doubt," Halas explained, "there was a hundred bucks in the whole room."

A year later, Halas' Decatur Staleys had moved to Chicago, the APFA had become the National Football League, and the evolutionary process that was to take the sport from virtual obscurity to a dominant position as America's number-one spectator sport had begun.

Television? Back in 1922, after Halas had re-

Pages 6–7: Pregame tensions mount as players wait for TV introductions at Super Bowl XV.

named the Staleys the Bears, television was as far from anyone's thoughts as a profit was from anyone's pockets. People still were learning about that "wireless" thing Guglielmo Marconi had invented that was just becoming commercial radio. It took another three dozen years for the marriage between the NFL and television to be consummated—and a short history of the relationship provides the necessary understanding for recognizing where the sport is now and where it is going during the eighties.

The link between professional football and television originally was forged in 1949 when the NFL championship game was first telecast on a special network. Not too many really cared at that historical juncture, but from then on, little by little, professional football and its stars—Otto Graham, Bobby Layne, Norm Van Brocklin, Lou Groza, Ollie Matson, Johnny Unitas—were introduced by the media more and more to a public obviously looking to adore sports heroes.

Television also provided the opportunity for fans to learn the game that seemed so complicated without visual explanation. At home, the fan received his explanation or, as one newly fascinated viewer of that era explained, "You watched a game on television and, suddenly, the wool was stripped from your eyes. What had appeared to be an incomprehensible tangle of milling bodies from the grandstand, made sense. It was the first real triumph of educational television. It created a nation of instant experts in no time."

The link between the NFL and TV, however, still needed a catalyst to provide the excitement in the marriage that made it seem like the two were made for each other from the first moment Halas sat down on a running board in Ralph Hays's showroom. It was provided by a guy who was as hungry to play the game as Halas was to organize it—Johnny Unitas, the crew-cut quarterback who was acquired by the Baltimore Colts for the price of an 80-cent phone call.

Unitas had joined the Pittsburgh Steelers in 1955 without much fanfare after finishing his college career at the University of Louisville; he had been released with even less fanfare. But he didn't quit, hooking up instead with the Bloomfield (Pennsylvania) Rams, so, when Weeb Ewbank needed a quarterback for the Colts in 1956, he was only an 80-cent phone call away.

By 1958, when he guided the Colts into the NFL championship game against the New York Giants, Unitas had become the prototype of the pro quarterback of the era—the Golden Arm able to launch a pass with pinpoint precision.

Those who know also insist that the man with the Golden Arm was driven by that first rejection slip. "The great ones never forget what it means to come up the hard way," says Norm Van Brocklin, a Hall of Famer like Unitas. "Unitas knows what it is to eat potato soup without the potatoes in it."

But, on December 28, 1958, Unitas made it a steak-and-potatoes wash-it-down-with-champagne day for himself, the Colts, even the losing Giants, and all of professional football. For the drama played out during that game at Yankee Stadium, with Unitas the star at center stage, indelibly etched the picture of the sport on the American psyche.

The sports public had heard and read about great games before, but television enabled them to see this overtime struggle for supremacy. Television was about to demonstrate that it was the perfect instrument with which to zoom in on the action and relay it to the fans' living rooms. It is exactly as Val Pinchbeck suggested—television was the perfect method for spotlighting professional football. And that 1958 championship game in which Unitas steered the Colts to victory was the vehicle that proved it.

It is no accident that the NFL had just 12 teams until Unitas and the Colts captured the nation's imagination; that during the next two decades the clamor for additions was so great that the total now stands at 28 with two more expected to follow, at least one in the 1980s. It is no accident that television is paying the NFL approximately $650 million for the four-year period ending in 1981 for the rights to televise its games, more than all the TV money paid to professional football from 1960 to 1977.

Television and its money is to the structure of the NFL today what Halas' APFA was in 1920—the base from which the league operates. Television money has turned $100 franchises into $20 million businesses and turned players who passed helmets for coins into millionaires.

The architect of the NFL's television policy—as he is of everything else in the NFL's realm—is commissioner Pete Rozelle, the 54-year-old former public relations director who fully understands the unique relationship between professional football and television.

He understands it—and has made it work for the NFL—so well that Bob Wussler, former president of CBS Sports, pays him this tribute: "I think the owners should build a marble statue to Pete Rozelle in Canton, Ohio [site of the Pro Football Hall

9

Above: *O. J. Simpson, a legendary running back on the field, interviewed by TV sportscaster Frank Gifford. Gifford has first-hand knowledge of the game. He is in the Pro Football Hall of Fame from his years with the Giants.* Top: *Pete Rozelle, NFL commissioner and architect of the creative relationship between the NFL and TV.* Right: *The game calls for controlled violence; sometimes control is lost.*

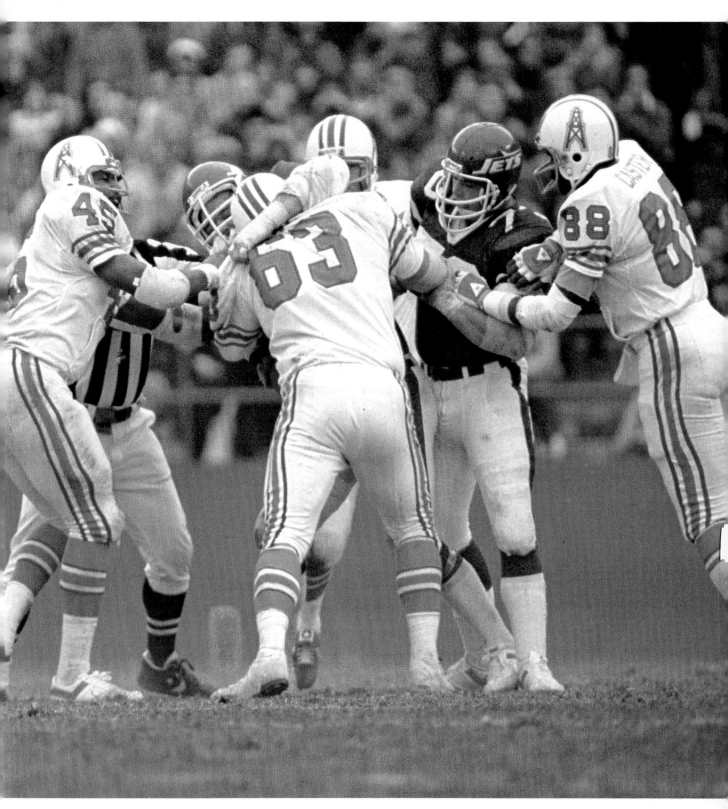

low the director to shoot as if you were actually in the stadium. You'll be able to see the whole field. I also think you'll see less announcing and more picture. You'll feel like you're right there in the crowd, and all you'll need are graphics and replays."

Chet Forte, director of ABC's Monday Night Football, concurs, at least jokingly, with Verna's view of announcing. "Don't tell Howard [Cosell], but I've always wanted to try a game with no announcers," Forte says.

(NBC conducted an experiment along those lines on December 19, 1980, televising a Miami Dolphins-New York Jets game at the Orange Bowl without announcers. Twelve microphones were set up in an attempt to fill the dead air, but most of the sounds were muffled. The network also used far more graphics than usual in an attempt to give the viewer background material.

Viewer reaction in the few polls taken was favorable, but the general reaction from critics was that the telecast was too difficult to follow without announcers.

Bum Phillips, coach of the Houston Oilers, said he would even prefer to listen to Howard Cosell than be left without any comment whatsoever. "At least," said Phillips, "you've got something to be mad at.")

"Cameras will be a lot smaller," Forte continues, "and we'll be able to get into positions we've never been able to get to before. I also think you'll see more overhead shots, not gimmick stuff, but really meaningful. You might also view the game from both end zones. That's a way-out possibility because people are so used to seeing it the other way. You'll see the holes open up, the receivers coming downfield at you. The possibilities are limitless."

The new technology available for telecasting will be focusing on a game that continues to change from the one telecast during the sixties and seventies. The biggest change, according to Tex Schramm, president of the Dallas Cowboys, will occur in the sphere of specialization. "The forty-five-man roster won't be thought of in terms of traditional positions, more in terms of players who have specific skills," Schramm forecasts. "Teams will be looking for guys who can do one certain thing on offense or defense real well.

"Clubs will get away from the traditional starting lineup. There will be pass-blocking specialists at the line—it's not a remote idea to think that your offensive line would use one combination for pass

of Fame] and everybody should have to bow down to it three times a day."

While they're chiseling that statue of Rozelle, the game will continue to change. It will have to do that to maintain its popularity with an adoring public that jams its stadiums; it will have to do that to remain a vibrant product for television to beam around the country and across the oceans.

Nothing, after all, stands still without stagnating. The NFL cannot afford that. And while acknowledging it, Rozelle points out he doesn't believe the NFL will change as drastically as it has in the last 20 years. "Maybe I'm not much of a visionary, but I can't envision the same sort of major changes over the next twenty years that we've had since 1960," Rozelle says. "I would say we'll probably be at thirty teams by then with five six-team divisions in each conference. I wouldn't think we could play any more than sixteen games. I don't see us playing worldwide. But I do think people will be seeing more professional football around the world as communications continue to improve."

The advance in communications will be significant, beginning with the way the game is telecast. "In twenty years, we'll all be watching games on huge screens, and that will totally change the concept as to how television shows the game," says CBS director Tony Verna. "The wide screen will al-

From an organizational meeting in a car showroom in Canton, Ohio to the ownership of the Chicago Bears, George Halas has been at the forefront of pro football's phenomenal growth for over 60 years.

blocking, another for run blocking—and other substitutions made for a particular play. We already have the short-yardage teams and the long-yardage teams utilizing players for specific purposes; now it will be carried to a further extent. The very last thing—and, maybe, it's not feasible—would be quarterbacks for certain situations.

"It will become more and more a chess game—where do you deploy the bishops and knights, when do you castle your rooks? Everything is getting more sophisticated. We're continuing to do more and more offensively and defensively."

That will require coaches and players who can operate securely on and survive the nuances of that chessboard. "It's not going to be a game for the unintelligent player or unintelligent coach," Schramm emphasizes. "It will be an era when there will be greater pressure than ever on the coaches. More decisions will be made on the move as reactions, just like they are now with the quarterback and receiver who have to read and react to the defense while the play is developing. The game will be far more demanding from an intellectual standpoint. The game is going to be more and more a game of specialists and individual plays. It will come down to having the right man in the right position doing the right thing at the right time."

Schramm also believes that electronic gear will enter into pro football in the 1980s with quarterbacks possibly wearing some form of listening device in their helmets that would enable them to hear plays called by the coach from the sidelines. "So many teams are calling plays from the sidelines, I don't see the harm in letting the quarterback have a transistor in his helmet," Schramm says. "It would speed up games. There wouldn't be any wig-wagging from the sidelines or sending in players to tell the quarterback the play."

Schramm, however, doesn't foresee too many rules changes, except in the area of safety. "There will be continued tightening of rules in the area of safety," Schramm says. "The public is turned off to violence and unnecessary roughness. There's always going to be injuries, but there will be more and closer regulation of acts that could bring about injury.

"We also must keep a fair balance between offense and defense. We're starting the 1980s with a pretty good balance, even though many people are saying the offense has too many advantages. But that's not really true as far as I'm concerned. Back in the 1960s, NFL scoring was at forty-three to forty-four points a game, then we went down to thirty-four points a game in 1977. That's when the rules were changed, the passing game took off, and we're back today where we were in the 1960s. We've gotten back to where scoring was when the game had its greatest rise, passing baseball and becoming the number-one sport."

Lamar Hunt, cofounder of the American Football League and owner of the Kansas City Chiefs, feels the passing arms of the NFL's offenses will become even more potent than they are now. "There are more quarterbacks coming out of college who are proficient passers," Hunt points out. "And our coaches are getting used to it. Teams are realizing they don't need the three- to four-yard running game to be successful."

Along those same lines, Hunt believes defenses trying to stop the new air-oriented offenses are being penalized far too often when they commit pass interference. "Any time you can be penalized up to 40 to 50 yards, that distorts anything," Hunt says. "Half the distance [of the pass] would be logical. That would negate those automatic touchdowns when there's interference in the end zone and the ball is placed on the one-yard line."

Hunt also favors three other proposed rules changes—making kickoff and punt returns mandatory and substituting a 25-second period for the 30-second period permitted for a team to get off a play.

Hunt sees so many kickoffs downed in the end zone and punts fair caught that he deplores the situation. "Those are exciting plays and skill is involved in doing both," Hunt says. "It seems kind of incongruous in a game that is so aggressive that you should be able to kneel [with a kickoff] in the end zone and down the ball. It's so different from the nature of the game."

Hunt is in favor of taking five seconds off the time a team has to run a play for a similar reason; he thinks the 30 seconds currently permitted slows the action. "The public enjoys a spontaneous game," Hunt points out. "There's too much time taken with thirty seconds to call a play. The game is more fun when it's unpredictable. I like the hurry-up aspect of the college game. They're not as proficient as the professionals, but the excitement they generate is tremendous."

Hank Stram, the former coach of the Chiefs, now a TV analyst, likes the college game too, particularly the option play. He predicts it will finally come into play during the 1980s on a significant basis. "People have toyed with it but no one has featured it," Stram says. "With more college coaches coming into the pros, coaches who have had suc-

Opposite: *Miami's ground attack tests the New York Jets' defensive line. Quick opening plays like this are much clearer to the fans because of TV isolation shots and instant replays.* Above: *Louie Giammona, 5'9" and 180 pounds, plays big for Philadelphia.*

cess with it, I think you'll see the option become an integral part of many offenses."

Stram also sees a continuation of the trend that began with Tom Landry at Dallas and himself at Kansas City during the 1970s. "Ten years ago, I said the seventies would be the decade of variety," Stram points out. "I think the 1980s and 1990s will be a progression of that—more teams doing more and more things on both offense and defense."

All of it—the new specialists, the new rules—will be subjected to the lens of the television camera, which has been the NFL's partner ever since it took over from radio. And that partnership will continue, despite those who feel overexposure is a threat to the sport.

"The fact that we are winning more and more fans is because of television," says Halas, who scorns those who talk of overexposure. "That [television] is the reason we will continue to grow in popularity. It seems that wherever we went we were accepted by fans, by radio, by television. We used radio first and then television to introduce our game to the fans. It's like sending a salesman ahead to show the people the product."

Halas likes to compare the use of radio and television as a method of promoting the product to the use of Red Grange when the sport was struggling in the early years after formation. The Galloping Ghost of collegiate fame quit the University of Illinois after playing his last college game in November 1925, signed with Halas' Bears, and immediately began a cross-country tour of 18 exhibition games, 8 in one 12-day stretch.

"It all started with Red Grange," Halas insists as he traces the growth of the sport in his mind. "Grange opened the doors to the public. He was then and still remains the most publicized player in history. He was in his day what radio and TV were to become later."

Grange made his debut in Chicago's Wrigley Field on Thanksgiving Day before a capacity crowd of 36,000. "If there was room we could have had another thirty thousand," Halas points out. "Then we went to New York and drew seventy-five thousand the day after the Army-Navy game only drew sixty. We went barnstorming to Florida, to St. Louis, and out to the West Coast. All along the way we had to keep stopping the train so people in remote areas of the country could get a glimpse of him. They knew the train was coming and they'd be out waiting."

That the sport survived is, indeed, a tribute to players like Grange and pioneers like Halas, whose

vision was sharp enough to anticipate the future, ignore the persistent problems of the present, and continue to struggle while teams appeared and disappeared with startling regularity.

Take the case of Detroit. The city had a team in 1920 and 1921, but it folded at that point. Detroit had a team again in 1925, but was out again in 1927. Detroit was in once more in 1928, but out once more in 1929. It wasn't until five years later—when the Portsmouth, Ohio, franchise was shifted to Detroit—that the city became a permanent member.

The 28-team structure that exists today is the result of 94 different team entities in 54 different locales. Only two teams have made the entire trip from 1920 to the present—Halas' Staleys and the Chicago Cardinals, now based in St. Louis.

It's difficult to conceive of so much franchise shifting during the current era of stability in which more than 13 million people fill stadiums to watch the NFL's 224-game regular-season schedule. The sport is so popular that when TV looked at its top sports shows of all time at the end of the seventies, the five telecasts at the top were the 1975 to 1979 Super Bowls. Eight of the all-time top ten were Super Bowls.

What makes the sport so appealing? The NFL asked a number of players and coaches that question for a book it published to honor itself on its fiftieth birthday. Two players—Washington Redskins quarterback Sonny Jurgensen and St. Louis Cardinals safety Larry Wilson—indicated they felt they performed a therapeutic service for the fans watching in the stands.

"I've always considered myself a group therapist for sixty thousand people," Jurgensen said. "Every Sunday I hold group therapy and the people come out and take out their frustrations on me. If I fail, it magnifies their failures, and if I succeed, it minimizes them."

"This," said Wilson, "is one way for people to release their aggressions. I see them coming out of the stands [after the game], they are wringing wet with sweat, they are mad, they have played a football game and they look as beat up as the football players on the field."

Two of the game's most celebrated coaches—Vince Lombardi and Paul Brown—also tried to explain the sport's popularity. "I think the nature of man is to be aggressive and football is a violent game," Lombardi said. "But I think the very violence is one of the great things about the game, because a man has to learn control. He is going to go

in to knock somebody's block off and yet he must keep rein on it. I can't think of any other place that demands such discipline."

"I've known women who thought football was worthless and brutal," Brown said. "But they just don't understand the sport and they don't understand the nature of the male. Most of those big collisions don't really hurt. The players are dressed and protected. They are young and strong. Anyway, the fact is that young men enjoy it. Nothing is going to stop it."

All players, however, don't see it through Brown's rose-tinted glasses. Merlin Olsen, former defensive tackle for the Los Angeles Rams, now a TV analyst, always insisted playing did hurt, and Ron Mix, a Hall of Fame tackle who played with the San Diego Chargers, says he never loved the sport.

"They don't call the middle of the line 'the Pit' for nothing," Olsen said while he still was playing. "We really do get like animals, trying to claw one another apart out there. We get so bruised and battered and tired we sometimes wind up playing in a sort of coma. By the end of the first half your instincts have taken over. By the end of the game you're an animal. When you come right down to it, your life is at stake out there."

"My attitude about football upset many people who think an athlete should love what he is doing," Mix says. "But I don't think an athlete should love his job any more than anybody else. The only important thing for an athlete to realize is that he has an obligation to do well. I've always realized that. If I could have loved the game besides, that would have been a little frosting on the cake. But that wasn't the case."

Why do they do it then? Money, of course, is a major reason. It's why George Halas went to work for A. E. Staley. And it's why Earl Campbell bangs into the line for the Houston Oilers and why Ron Jaworski stands in the pocket and throws a pass for the Philadelphia Eagles while defensive linemen crash into his body.

And money could be one problem area for the NFL in the 1980s. The average NFL salary at the end of the seventies was $68,893, well below the average in the other three major professional sports—baseball, basketball, and hockey. It's obvious that NFL players could, at any time, stage a revolt either individually or collectively in an attempt to catch up with their colleagues in other sports.

Here's the way those 1979 salary figures looked in three different surveys.

John Matuszak, the Raiders' awesome 6'5", 280-pound defensive end, is a study in concentration as he gets a breather. Oakland built a Super Bowl XV victory around veteran players like Matuszak.

17

Left: *The highest paid player of the seventies, O. J. Simpson (32), put out of the driver's seat in a play against Detroit.* Below: *Franco Harris, a premiere NFL rusher.* Opposite: *Bell (42), Giles (88), and Davis (38) are building a young Tampa team.*

Top Salaries

1. O. J. Simpson, San Francisco 49ers, running back	$806,668
2. Walter Payton, Chicago Bears, running back	450,000
3. Bob Griese, Miami Dolphins, quarterback	400,025
4. Archie Manning, New Orleans Saints, quarterback	379,000
5. Dan Pastorini, Houston Oilers, quarterback	358,333
6. Chuck Foreman, Minnesota Vikings, running back	300,000
John Riggins, Washington Redskins, running back	300,000
8. Ken Stabler, Oakland Raiders, quarterback	282,000
9. Bert Jones, Baltimore Colts, quarterback	275,000
Franco Harris, Pittsburgh Steelers, running back	275,000
Delvin Williams, Miami Dolphins, running back	275,000

Top-Paid Players, By Position

Running back—O. J. Simpson, San Francisco 49ers	$806,668
Quarterback—Bob Griese, Miami Dolphins	400,025
Receiver—Russ Francis, New England Patriots	202,333
Offensive lineman—Gene Upshaw, Oakland Raiders	150,000
Art Shell, Oakland Raiders	150,000
Defensive lineman—Lee Roy Selmon, Tampa Bay Buccaneers	218,000
Linebacker—Isaiah Robertson, Buffalo Bills	230,000
Defensive back—Willie Buchanon, San Diego Chargers	175,000
Kicker—Russell Erxleben, New Orleans Saints	110,714

Average Salaries, By Position

Quarterbacks	$113,932
Running backs	74,194
Receivers	64,631
Offensive linemen	66,584
Defensive linemen	75,246
Linebackers	63,377
Defensive backs	58,874
Kickers	53,030
All players	68,893

Veteran members of the Los Angeles Rams did stage a mini-revolt prior to the 1980 season when it was learned that the club had signed its number-one draft choice—defensive back Johnny Johnson of Texas—to a multiyear contract for more than $1 million. Now, it should be noted that several baseball players earn in the neighborhood of $1 million a year, although that list admittedly is short. Going into 1980, pitcher Nolan Ryan of the Houston Astros, third-baseman George Brett of the Kansas City Royals, and outfielder Dave Parker of the Pittsburgh Pirates were on the list.

There are several other potential problem areas for the sport in the future: criticism of violence in the game, accusations of racial discrimination, and the threat of gambling. That professional football is a violent sport is documented by any number of players. The subject of violence, however, is getting more of a public airing than ever before and the result could be damaging to pro football's image.

"I'm not sure the game is rougher today than

it used to be," Tex Schramm says, "but the roughness is being talked about more. We're coming into an era when undue violence is repelling people. This isn't just an NFL finding. My friends in television and the movies tell me brutality isn't the salable quality it used to be. There has been a public reaction against an excessive amount of violent scenes. Sports fans today differentiate between contact and brutality."

Any solution creates a problem because it centers around the question of what to do without changing the basic nature of the game. In a campaign aimed at educating the people in the sport, Rozelle has fined players for acts he considers excessive.

"You can change the attitude of players, coaches, and others interested in football," Schramm says. "Everybody knows what unnecessary roughness is. All you need is a general understanding—an agreement—that going too far will be punished."

An even more damaging public relations problem is the accusation being made that the NFL has limited the ability of black players to rise to management positions. The most recent stir was caused by a study commissioned by the NFL Players Association and made by a Johns Hopkins researcher.

Dr. Jomills Braddock II, of the Johns Hopkins Center for Social Organization of Schools, compiled data on more than 5,000 players who were in the NFL from 1960 through 1979. That data showed that there were no black head coaches in the NFL and in the previous 20 years there had been only 20 black assistant coaches. During that same period of time, Braddock pointed out, 261 assistants and 69 head coaches were hired from the ranks of former players.

"We found strong suggestions that race does matter in managerial recruitment in professional football," Braddock concluded. "Race exerted a larger direct or independent effect than three other predicators—educational attainment, central positional assignment [having been a quarterback, center, guard, or linebacker], and the player's professional accomplishments."

Rozelle's answer to charges such as these has been to categorically deny that the NFL discriminates against blacks. "To say that the National Football League is discriminatory is absolutely ludicrous," Rozelle usually insists. Then he points out that the same kind of charges could be made against other businesses.

It's obvious that there really is no completely satisfactory answer to the charge other than employment of blacks in management roles—and the prospect is that during the 1980s qualified blacks will begin to take over more positions in the front office and that there will be black head coaches. Pro basketball and major league baseball long ago broke the color line when it came to hiring a black head coach or manager and there's no question the NFL will have to follow.

While violence and the subject of racial discrimination are problems that can be solved internally, the problem of gambling cannot. The NFL has always been opposed to proposals for the legalization of gambling on professional team sports, and thus far has been able to win the battle. The threat is always present, however, and begins to loom considerably larger with the establishment of betting casinos in Atlantic City, New Jersey. The possibility certainly exists that other cities will follow suit and pursue the legalization of sports betting.

The league's posture is simple, as stated by Rozelle during the 1980 season: "The league traditionally has been opposed to various referendums which would create state-run casinos and gambling houses similar to those recently established in New Jersey. We fear that eventually there will be enormous pressure to place sports betting right alongside roulette wheels, crap games, and slot machines in these gambling houses. By turning sports events into betting events, it would cast shadows over the very integrity of professional team sports."

Gambling is not a threat to be taken lightly, and there's little doubt that Rozelle and the NFL will continue to fight it.

Meanwhile, Rozelle will be looking to solidify the gains made in his first 20 years as commissioner. But, in addition to solidifying, he will be prepared to make advances that would put the NFL in the unchallenged role as number one among all team sports. "Now's the chance," Rozelle says, "for pro football to surpass all other sports in the country. To be at the top."

That would be fun for every owner, including George Halas. But Halas doesn't really need that kind of status to fully enjoy what he's still doing more than 60 years after he helped get it all started.

All George Halas needs to be happy is one win a week. "I still love the game because it's so great," Halas says. "If your team wins a football game, you feel great all week. If you go out and have a couple of drinks, you feel good, too, but that only lasts a couple of hours."

2

Passing Into the Eighties

Sid Gillman left the University of Cincinnati in 1955 to take over as coach of the Los Angeles Rams, bringing with him his ever-present pipe, the bow ties that bobbed on his Adam's apple, and the realization that he had a major gap in his education.

"I knew so little about the pro passing game that I decided I just had to make a career out of it," Gillman says. "I couldn't wait until the season ended so I could get back to work and find out how you put together a pro passing game. It has been a great interest to me ever since—the art of making moves and fooling individuals . . . the art of putting designs together so the quarterback has good reads . . . what you can do to coordinate everything with the drop of the quarterback."

It was that thirst for knowledge which led Sid Gillman to do the painstaking research that gave birth to his theories of full-field passing and made him the father of the modern passing game in the National Football League.

"I studied films," Gillman explains. "Everything comes from films. We couldn't have any kind of game without them. I probably have the biggest library of anybody. We have some people in our profession who are scientists, researchers. Fortunately, I was brought up that way.

"I used to work for a coach who put me on the right track from the word go. His name was Francis Schmidt. He was the head coach at Ohio State University, and I was on his staff for four years. Schmidt was brilliant. He was the Van Gogh of football. There is nobody I've come in contact with, before or since, that had his knowledge and ability to work. He taught me there was no such thing as a clock. He taught me to become a worker, a searcher."

The searcher found most of his source material in all those films and the exceptional talent right in front of him on the Rams' practice field. "I had [Norm] Van Brocklin, who was a great, great passer," Gillman points out. "And we had some great ends—Tom Fears, who was one of the great 'move'

men in the business, and Elroy Hirsch. I'd talk to them, but just watching the moves they made gave me all sorts of ideas."

With all that funneled into his mind ("No one person influenced me," Gillman says, "it was everybody"), the searcher turned into an innovator and decided that a team didn't have to establish the run in order to be able to pass. A pro team could succeed doing the exact opposite. "My theories," Gillman explains, "are predicated on a team being able to throw the ball, forcing that team to use full-field formations which lend themselves to passing. From that, you utilize all running available."

Oddly, Gillman never really had the opportunity to fully test those theories in the NFL as it existed at the time. Before long, Vince Lombardi's run-to-daylight theories had become the basis for virtually all coaching philosophies in the NFL and Gillman had moved on to coach in the American Football League. It was in the AFL, with the San Diego Chargers, that Gillman finally and fully implemented his theories, not only because he wanted to, but also because he had to.

Needing names to fill its stadiums, the AFL outbid the NFL in signing the top offensive stars coming out of college. That made the AFL far more offensive-oriented than the NFL and far more likely to experiment with the passing game. "We had to throw the ball," Gillman says. "Nobody had any great defenses. And we had to appeal. I thought that the AFL, from that standpoint, had a slight advantage. When you start something new, people want to see the ball. They don't care where it goes, as long as you put it in the air."

That they did in the AFL. What Gillman began, others continued. One of Gillman's assistants at San Diego was Al Davis, who went on to coach at Oakland and install the long-range passing attack the Raiders have always favored.

Another Charger assistant was Chuck Noll, who eventually took over the Pittsburgh Steelers. Noll started his career with a run-oriented offense revolving around Franco Harris, then went to the

Preceding pages: The Jets' Richard Todd releases the ball before the pass rush can get to him. Opposite: The Seattle Seahawks' Jim Zorn is one of the young quarterbacks to watch in the eighties.

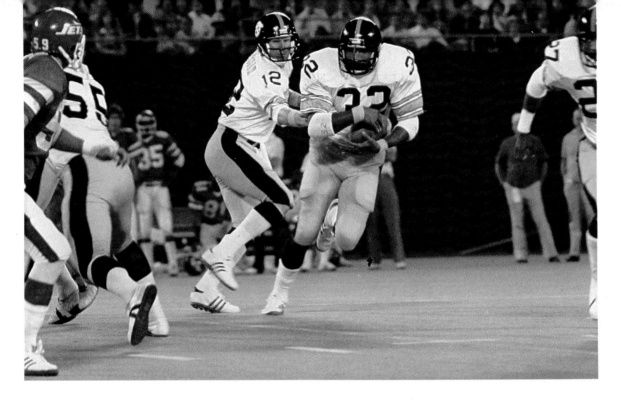

air with Terry Bradshaw firing deep downfield to Lynn Swann and John Stallworth. It is that kind of total commitment to the philosophy of full-field passing boldly applied to the pro game by Gillman that is at the heart of the passing revolution continuing to develop in the NFL.

If there was any question that there has been a revolution in the way the game is played in the NFL, it was totally dispelled on the tenth weekend of the 1980 season when 732 points were scored. It was the highest one-week total in the entire 61-year history of the league and was built on a number of exceptional passing and receiving performances. The explosion had been anticipated ever since the beginning of the 1978 season when the rules were liberalized, paving the way for coaches to take advantage of the theories advanced by Gillman and his disciples.

The fuse, however, had burned slowly as pass-oriented coaches experimented with the new rules and run-oriented coaches started to change their emphasis. Finally, on November 9 and 10, 1980, nine quarterbacks threw for 300 or more yards and 12 receivers gained 100 or more yards while the NFL's computers rang up 732 points. The palace had been stormed, the revolution completed.

The statistical evidence supporting that contention was overwhelming, underscoring how much more effective the NFL's air arms had become in just three seasons. Here are some examples:

• Through the 10-week period capped by the 732-point explosion, 714 touchdowns had been scored, 141 more than in 1977. More than half—55 percent—came on passes.

• The 392 passing touchdowns represented an increase of 128—or almost one-third—over 1977.

• Passing yardage was averaging 400.5 yards a game, an increase of 44 percent or 122.6 yards a game over 1977.

These amazing increases came after a 1979 season which in itself had been eye-opening, as it ushered in the decade of the 1980s. In 1977, there had been just five 300-yard passing games put together by NFL quarterbacks. In 1978, there were 15. And, then, in 1979, the total mushroomed to 44. From 1971 to 1977, just 10 receivers gained 1,000 yards or more in a season. In 1979, 12 did it.

That 1979 barrage of 300-yard passing games and 1,000-yard receivers certainly emphasized the changes the sport was undergoing, but there were other signs, including the following:

• Dan Fouts of the San Diego Chargers passed for an NFL record 4,082 yards.

• Steve Largent of the Seattle Seahawks gained 1,237 yards receiving, the highest total since Warren Wells of the Oakland Raiders gained 1,260 in 1969.

• Ahmad Rashad of the Minnesota Vikings caught 80 passes, becoming the first wide receiver to reach that plateau since Lionel Taylor of the

Above: Bradshaw (12) deals to Harris (32), a Steeler trademark in the seventies. Opposite: Dan Fouts (14) connected for a record 4,082 yards in 1979. Receivers Jefferson, Joiner, and Winslow each made over 1,000 yards in receptions.

Denver Broncos in 1965.

The revolution has not only changed the nature of the game, but has started to create a group of new headliners—the wide receivers. Flying downfield to latch onto a spiral or leaping high into the air to corral a pass, they will certainly be the glamour boys of the eighties.

Forget the running backs. Forget the pass rushers. Forget the quarterbacks. Watch those wide receivers. Watch John Jefferson and Charley Joiner of the San Diego Chargers. Watch Harold Carmichael of the Philadelphia Eagles. Watch Stanley Morgan and Harold Jackson of the New England Patriots. Watch Pat Tilley of the St. Louis Cardinals.

Watch Tony Hill of the Dallas Cowboys, James Lofton of the Green Bay Packers, Jerry Butler of the Buffalo Bills, Wes Chandler of the New Orleans Saints, and Wesley Walker of the New York Jets. Not to mention Largent and Rashad and a cast that continues to grow.

The San Diego receivers are so proficient within the framework of Don Coryell's wide-open passing attack—it's dubbed Air Coryell—that defenders who have to try to stop them come away stunned by their ability.

"Dan Fouts was right on the mark with most of his passes," said Philadelphia linebacker Frank LeMaster after the Eagles had played the Chargers. "If there'd been a cold out there in the stands, their receivers probably would've caught that, too." "Their receivers are like poetry in motion," said another Eagles' linebacker, Jerry Robinson. "Those guys were born with magnets in their hands."

Besides Jefferson and Joiner, the Chargers have an excellent tight end in Kellen Winslow. Each member of the San Diego trio collected 1,000 yards receiving during the 1980 season—becoming the first threesome in history to achieve that kind of success.

Why are there suddenly so many outstanding receivers? "I think the influence of television on young people and young coaches has been considerable," says Raymond Berry, who used to catch Johnny Unitas' passes and is now an assistant coach in charge of the New England Patriots' receivers. "When you see the wide receivers and the passing game on TV, it's a big motivating factor in a youngster wanting to play that position or a coach wanting to use that type of offense."

Berry also points out that many of the receivers have added an extra dimension to pass-catching that hasn't always been utilized—leaping. "Many of today's receivers are leapers and jumpers," Berry notes. "It's always been an effective way of catching but has never been acknowledged. People say you got to grab the ball with your hands. Those guys jump up and catch it with everything they have."

Finally, Berry emphasizes, wide receivers today are benefiting from opportunities the pass-catchers of another era didn't always have. "Receivers today are getting maximum opportunity to use their abilities," Berry says. "Many great receivers [in the past] didn't get the numbers because of the system in which they played. Paul Warfield played the big part of his career with Miami when they threw the ball twelve times a game."

Don Shula at Miami and, before him, Vince Lombardi at Green Bay became legends in their own time by passing the ball as few as 12 times a game while utilizing the running game to its fullest. Lombardi got the job done with Jim Taylor and Paul Hornung and a quarterback in Bart Starr whose major role was handing off to those two receivers. Bob Griese performed the same function for Shula, tucking the ball into Larry Csonka's midsection or giving it to either Jim Kiick or Mercury Morris.

While Lombardi was winning two Super Bowls and Shula was winning two Super Bowls, other coaches were rapidly copying what they were doing and turning out carbon copies—teams that relied on ball control and defense to win games. As a result of all the ball-control offenses and the strong defenses developed to stop them in a tug-of-war between massive men along the line of scrimmage, there was an appreciable drop in scoring that began to frighten the NFL's owners.

There was the threat of declining attendance in low-scoring games, and the owners were quick to recognize it. "I've never received one letter complaining about too much scoring," says Tex Schramm, president of the Dallas Cowboys and a member of the NFL's competition committee that changed the rules. "I've got tons of mail about officiating. But never about too much scoring. Fans don't want to see defense. They want to see offense."

Schramm also points out that the NFL's greatest period of growth occurred during the 1960s when scoring was at a peak. "I think the high [for scoring] was around 1964–65," Schramm says. "But it [more scoring] began in the early 1950s—teams started using three receivers and the defensive backs just couldn't cover them man-to-man. The Rams started it all, with Elroy Hirsch and

Glenn Davis—they made everybody change."

While Schramm was arguing for more scoring, people like Shula and Noll favored the status quo. "I'm from a defensive background," explains Shula, who was a defensive back as a player. "My position was that I wanted to keep the rules the way they were."

"I'm in the entertainment business, I realize that," Noll admits. "If you want to punch some more points on the scoreboard, I'm for it. But I prefer a long drive to a quick touchdown. We've got to be careful not to make a touch football game out of it."

Despite those pleas, the owners felt compelled to help the offenses. In 1978, the new rules went into effect, handcuffing the defense by eliminating the bump-and-run technique after a receiver is five yards downfield.

In the 1950s, a defensive back for the St. Louis Cardinals, Jimmy Hill, was among the first to realize that the best way to stop a receiver from being able to run his route was to hit him as he came off the line of scrimmage and keep banging away at him as he ran downfield—to intimidate and/or throw him off stride. In the AFL, where Gillman's passing philosophies were being adopted by others and forging an air-minded league, the bump-and-run became the prime counter-weapon. The Oakland Raiders, with Kent McCloughan and Willie Brown, made it a way of life.

The rules makers, looking to increase scoring, decided that the bump-and-run was so effective that it had to go. A defender would be permitted only one bump, and that within five yards of the line of scrimmage. Once the receiver got outside the five-yard area, he was free to roam without worrying about being hit by a defensive back.

At the same time, the rules concerning blocking by offensive linemen were liberalized, giving guards and tackles more weapons with which to fend off defenders trying to reach the quarterback before he can find a receiver and complete the pass. The liberalized rules paved the way for more scoring by enabling air-minded coaches like Coryell to take advantage of them and by forcing coaches such as Noll to convert from running to passing in order to be competitive.

What occurred on the tenth weekend of the 1980 season—that orgy of scoring—was the result. And everyone knows it. "This," said Hank Stram, "is the era of fast-break football. The quarterbacks come off the bus throwing." Stram should know. He is the former coach of the Kansas City Chiefs and New Orleans Saints who has become a TV analyst. He directed the Chiefs to their Super Bowl IV victory with a multifaceted attack he termed the "offense of the seventies."

"The cycle has changed," Stram says. "Coaches used to say it would be perfect balance to run the ball forty times and pass it twenty times a game. Now it actually is more like fifty-fifty, and the passes will increase. The NFL talked about wanting more entertainment. It has been accomplished. What we have is more excitement—big-play, fast-break football. Football goes in cycles. You had an accent on offense, the defense caught up with it, and the rules were changed favoring the offense."

And, what would Stram do to stop the offenses of the eighties if he were a defensive coach? "Pray more," he quipped.

On the other side of the ledger is George Allen, former coach of the Los Angeles Rams and Washington Redskins who is also a TV analyst. While the offensive-minded Stram snickers at what's happening, the defensive-oriented Allen laments the changes. "They're cheapening the game and it is only starting," Allen says. "Pro football scores are getting to be like high school basketball. It's gotten so now that all the coaches have to pass more. They see the other team doing it and if you don't want to lose, you've got to pass."

Allen isn't the only one who is upset with what's going on. It's so difficult to defend against the pass in the NFL today that coaches like Bum Phillips, formerly of the Houston Oilers and now with the New Orleans Saints, are beginning to wonder whether they have tipped the scales too far in one direction.

"It's harder to get to the quarterback [because of the way linemen can use their hands]," Phillips says. "It's harder to play defense when a guy gets five yards downfield and you can't touch him. I'd rather have a guy have a chance to defend himself on defense. I don't like to see a guy run down the field and come across the middle, and you can't touch him. That's not the way I was raised. You always made 'em pay the price for coming across the middle, don't you reckon?"

Ron Erhardt, the coach of the New England Patriots, reckons he'll have to agree with George Allen—if one team passes and wins, there will quickly be teams that duplicate their playing style. "Coaches and teams tend to copy coaches and teams who win," says Erhardt. "Back six and seven years ago, they were all running the ball because

29

that's what Miami was doing with [Larry] Csonka and [Jim] Kiick and they won it all. Now coaches are starting to look around and see that teams are winning by throwing the ball and so they're doing it, too. Either way, I don't care. I'm not married to the run and I'm not married to the pass. Whatever moves the ball best, I'll go with it."

Under the current rules, it has to be the pass, insists Raymond Berry. "There's no doubt the offense has the better of it," he says. "To me, the biggest factor is the legalized holding in the offensive line. The offensive blockers are using the same techniques they were using five or ten years ago. They were illegal then but eventually they became legal."

While Erhardt is leaning toward the pass in New England, run-oriented Dick Vermeil has become a convert in Philadelphia and enabled Sid Gillman to come out of the closet reserved for aging, former coaches.

Gillman was hired by Vermeil to supply some pizzazz for the Eagles' offense. He did it by resurrecting his passing theories and convincing Vermeil a team can control the ball with the pass as well as the run.

"By nature," says quarterback Ron Jaworski, "we're a conservative team. But now, everything has a big-play design. Our approach to the offensive

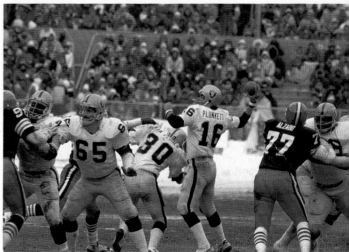

Opposite: *Ron Jaworski's arm put the Philadelphia Eagles into Super Bowl XV.* Above: *Jim Plunkett in the pocket against Cleveland. His passing took Oakland all the way in 1980.* Top: *Williams (29), Jefferson (83), and Smith (84) root for the Chargers.*

31

Top: *Vince Lombardi at Super Bowl I. Lombardi's theories took Bart Starr and his Green Bay Packers to two consecutive Super Bowl wins.* Above: *Quarterback Bart Starr carrying out the theories.*

game has been more aggressive. It's pretty obvious he's innovated the offense. The plays are basically the same we've been running for a couple of years now, but we have different formations and different people in different routes. That's the specific kind of thing that Sid contributed.

"We had all these things before. We just never used them," Jaworski continues. "Now we're varying the formations and that can look very drastic to a defense. All of a sudden, [running back] Wilbert Montgomery is out there on the flank and they're not sure what we're going to do off it.

"It reminds you of the teams Sid had in San Diego. They were all very aggressive offensively. And they all worked on the idea of efficient passing. But more than just giving his concept of offense to the players, I think he's given it to coach Vermeil. I think coach realizes now that Sid has gotten Joe [Pisarcik] and me ready to handle anything a defense throws against us. So coach Vermeil has gained confidence that his quarterbacks can handle any situation that comes up."

There is no doubt left by Vermeil as to where he stands. He admits he's a convert, and Gillman is the man who did it. "Working with Sid Gillman," Vermeil says, "is like going to the University of Pennsylvania and taking graduate courses. I think I'm a knowledgeable coach, but when you ask Sid a question and he gives you an answer, you know it's based on many years of experience."

The biggest gains, however, haven't been made by the converts; they've been made by those who already were believers in full-field passing. "The rule used to be that if you establish a running game first, the passing game will come along," Schramm points out. "Teams such as San Diego and San Francisco have reversed that, and these rules have helped. They've really gone overboard in making the pass their staple."

The Chargers and 49ers have gone so far overboard because of their coaches—Don Coryell and Bill Walsh. Both were committed to the pass long before the rule changes; the rules have only enhanced their strategic design. As a matter of fact, Coryell was having the ball thrown around as a college coach at San Diego State in the early 1960s at the same time, just a few miles away, Sid Gillman was perfecting his passing theories with the San Diego Chargers.

Coryell came to coaching in a roundabout way, and could just as easily have wound up as a boxer. After graduating from high school, Coryell was a paratrooper with an army ski unit, rising to

first lieutenant before he was discharged and entered the University of Washington. He played defensive back for the Huskies and also mixed it up in the boxing ring.

Coryell won all his fights as a light-heavyweight and displayed such skill the university asked him to remain on as an instructor. Coryell, however, decided to box professionally—a decision that eventually made him a coach. Boxing a heavyweight in a Seattle gym while weighing only 164 pounds, Coryell held his own until a punch separated his ribs. He began his college coaching career at Whittier College in California.

Coryell moved from Whittier to San Diego State for the 1961 season and compiled a 104–91–2 record. He then wrote a letter to owner Bill Bidwell of the St. Louis Cardinals and placed his name in nomination for the coaching job with the NFL club. Bidwell hired him. At St. Louis, where he refined his offensive thinking with the Jim Hart-Terry Metcalf Cardiac Cardinals, Coryell had a losing season in 1973, then ran off 10–4, 11–3, and 10–4 records while winning two NFC East titles. But he and Bidwell agreed to disagree during the 1977 season.

The next year, four games into the season, San Diego traded a draft choice to St. Louis for the right to hire Coryell as its coach, bringing the pass-conscious Coryell to the same team that had given the innovative Gillman his chance for full expression. No one, however, ever has succeeded at it like Coryell, with Dan Fouts firing passes all over the field to a corps of receivers that just might be the best in the business—John Jefferson, Charley Joiner, and Kellen Winslow, the NFL's only 1,000-yard triumvirate.

And it would appear that Coryell's philosophy, in part at least, stems from his boxing experiences. "I'm not a counterpuncher," he says, in laying out his philosophy. "There is nothing more boring than watching two counterpunchers fight. I don't want to wait for something to happen. Defensively and offensively, I believe in making something happen."

Coryell believes the best way to accomplish that is by throwing the ball. So he does, even when everyone knows that's exactly what the Chargers are going to do, or as quarterback Dan Fouts puts it, "We're going to throw the ball, and we don't care who knows it."

What are the key elements in the Chargers' passing attack? "We're always looking for the bomb," Fouts explains. "That's what's different [between us and other teams]. Long passing is built into our system. If they give it to us, we'll take a shot. But, when necessary, we're also geared to play conservative football. We have all the ball-control passes and runs and practice them as much as we practice anything. But if they take away our ball control on one side, we'll bomb the other side. Most teams don't pass that way. It's a question of looking for it. We're more conscious of taking a shot for a touchdown than other teams."

While the bomb tends to be more entertaining than the short pass, Coryell says his philosophy doesn't even take that into consideration. "When you need a hundred passes to win, we'll throw a hundred," he says. "When five passes are the best way to win, we'll only throw five, as we did one day in St. Louis. The only way to entertain is win."

And the best way to win, Coryell believes, is to have the pass as the major weapon in your arsenal. "I believe in it," he says. "I'm not a coach who builds on defense."

It's a philosophy that began to take shape when he took over at San Diego State. Most of the bigger and better linemen wound up going to USC or UCLA, so Coryell figured his best chance was to throw over people rather than run over them.

"If you have an average team and you can't throw the ball well, then you can't beat someone who's a lot better than you are," Coryell explains. "But if you are an average team or even a weak team and you have a fine passer and some fine receivers, sometimes you can go out and beat that better team.

"Over the years, I've had some pretty good teams, but there were some games I was going to lose when I had a rushing team. There was no doubt I was going to lose. We were not strong enough or good enough to compete.

"It's all right for a physically superior team to play conservatively and run over its opponents, but how many teams can do that? If you're playing a team with more talent, the only way to win is by throwing the ball well."

Coryell's team does that. And, even while the Chargers' ability to succeed with the pass has been enhanced by the new rules, Coryell continues to push for adoption of further changes that would help passing teams. He prefers the college possession rule on sideline receptions (one foot in bounds) to the NFL rule (two feet in bounds) and he is in favor of widening the field to "open up the game."

Walsh, like Coryell, was a college boxer, winning 18 of 21 bouts as a light-heavyweight for San Jose State, but he doesn't like to discuss those days. "I don't like to talk about my boxing career," he says, "because people kid me a lot about it." Walsh also played football at San Jose State but, unlike Coryell, was on offense, either as a halfback or an end. He was also a guard for the basketball team. But it was football that grabbed his attention.

Walsh got his start coaching high school in Fremont, California. He then became a perennial assistant, on the college level at the University of California and Stanford, and on the pro level at Oakland, Cincinnati, and San Diego. Wherever he went, there were rave reviews about his offensive design, but no head coaching offers.

Finally, disillusioned with the NFL after failing to get a head coaching post, he left the pro ranks when Stanford called to hand him its head coaching reins. Then, in 1979, the 49ers offered him the job he had been seeking for so many years. He left Stanford.

Walsh is held in such high esteem as an offensive thinker that, just after he was hired by the 49ers, he lectured the more than 1,000 members of the American Football Coaches Association on "Controlling the Ball with the Passing Game." When asked to profile himself, Walsh said, "I thrive on the technical aspects of football. I always have. I consider myself an excellent teacher and motivator, but above and beyond that I think that from a technical standpoint I might have more talent, more artistic capacity in that area than some others have."

He has a number of thoughts about passing and his role in its design. Here's a short collection.

On TD Passes: "If you take ten touchdown passes, five should end up exactly as we designed them. Three more will go to alternative receivers, and we have those for every play. The other two succeed because of greater effort by people who are putting out just a little more."

On Being Creative: "New plays don't just drop from heaven. They derive from a coach's knowledge of the game, an examination of all the equations possible, a conception of what is available from the human body within the rules, an appraisal of the opponent, an analysis of possible circumstances, and an examination of the chances for success."

On Quarterbacks: "The performance of a quarterback must be manipulated. To a degree, coaching can make a quarterback and it certainly is the most important factor for his success. The design of a team's offense is the key to a quarterback's per-

Dick Vermeil, head coach of the Philadelphia Eagles, says Sid Gillman convinced him to structure the offense around a full-field passing attack. Gillman's theories have now come of age.

formance. If you present a quarterback with an offensive script not suited to his overall makeup, he won't be able to survive, even with superior skills."

Walsh believes in attacking defenses with "everything you can do within the rules," but he isn't about to concede that the current emphasis on passing is merely a by-product of the rules changes. He feels coaches, notably himself, have made a significant contribution. "Right now offenses are dominating and defenses are at a disadvantage, which is a change from three or four years ago," he says, "but rules changes have not made the difference. We have new ways of attacking, new innovations. I know a lot of the things we did at Cincinnati [when he was an assistant with the Bengals] have brought some of it about—the method of formations and men in motion, for example. All across the league I see it now."

What about the new rules, Bill? "With the deep zones teams play, it's still awfully hard to complete the streak pass," he replies. "Teams put their two ball-hawking safeties deep and they cut off the bomb. But the new rules do give quarterbacks more time and receivers more time to maneuver. I see medium-range crossing patterns as the toughest passes to defend, but those patterns still put a premium on speed."

Walsh believes speed is one of the most important factors for a team that wants to revolve its offense around the pass. "It's so vital," Walsh emphasizes. "Whether he [the blazing fast receiver] catches a lot of balls or not isn't important. It's what someone like that can do to stress a defense. If you don't have the man who can extend the defense you have difficulty moving the ball."

Walsh also believes speed will be one of the answers for defenses trying to stop today's offenses. "Defensive linemen and linebackers will be slimmer in this decade and quicker," he predicts. "There will be less of a premium on big, physical players. And there will be even more of an emphasis on running backs who can catch the ball coming out of the backfield."

He feels so strongly about that because he believes in a high-percentage passing game, insisting the quarterback drop the ball off to the backs if he can't find a receiver downfield.

And there are those who believe that whatever Bill Walsh believes will succeed in the NFL. One of them is John Brodie, a former 49ers' quarterback now a TV analyst. "He's years ahead of most coaches," Brodie notes. "I don't know anybody who can match his knowledge of football."

There may not be too many in that category, but it should be pointed out that Walsh entered the eighties with just two pro wins to his credit, although he began to develop his passing attack in 1980 by installing Joe Montana at quarterback. Walsh and Coryell, who altogether had amassed 62 wins in seven NFL seasons going into 1980, may be the two coaches most in command of unique passing theories and, therefore, most capable of dealing with the strategic situation as it now exists.

But there are three coaches who managed to do during the seventies whatever was necessary to win. They are Don Shula, Chuck Noll, and Tom Landry, and expectations are that they will be able to mold teams that are fully competitive no matter what rules are being used.

Landry, of course, always has been a proponent of multiple offenses and Noll did begin to favor the pass when Terry Bradshaw matured. Even Shula, after he lost Larry Csonka and Jim Kiick, leaned on his passing game more until Bob Griese began to show signs of age.

All three of those masterminds also will be looking to climb up the all-time coaching standings by adding to their victory totals during the 1980s. Heading into the decade, Landry stood in third place all-time, with Shula fourth and Noll thirteenth among only 15 coaches who have won 100 or more games.

The all-time leader is George Halas with 326 wins, including both regular-season and postseason action. Earl ("Curly") Lambeau is second at 234, with Landry (187) and Shula (185) bidding to overtake him. Noll started 1980 with 114 wins, and was the only four-time Super Bowl winner.

Shula, Landry, Noll, and every other coach in the NFL will be striving in the 1980s not only to take advantage of the liberalized rules favoring passing but also to devise defensive alignments to counter the wide-open offenses.

And Tex Schramm of the Cowboys, one of those on the competition committee responsible for the current rules, knows that they will find the weapons to compete against the Coryells and Walshes. He knows it because he believes in the lessons of history. "During the late 1960s, NFL teams averaged more than forty points a game," Schramm notes. "We're just going back to where we were before the defenses became so big and quick. And, historically, the defense always catches up. You'll see, they'll figure something out."

Wide receivers like Philadelphia's Harold Carmichael have brought added excitement to the game. The speed, leaping ability, and body control of today's gifted receivers produce spectacular catches and higher scores.

3

Hallmarks of Excellence

Back in the late 1960s, when Joe Namath was still Broadway Joe, the New York Jets found themselves looking for a practice site while Shea Stadium underwent repairs. Coach Weeb Ewbank decided it would be Riker's Island, an island in the East River which just happened to house a 600-inmate prison.

On their first trip to the island, provision was made for the prisoners to watch the Jets work out. The inmates were kept behind ropes while armed guards looked on, but there was no trouble—except for the commotion caused by Namath's absence.

"Where's Joe?" yelled one prisoner from the sidelines. "Wouldn't [commissioner] Rozelle let him come out here?" That wasn't the case, the prisoner was told. Namath had to stay behind at the Jets' Shea Stadium quarters to take whirlpool treatments for his ailing left knee. "I have a bad knee, too," said the prisoner, "but they had me out here this morning mowing the grass so these Jets could practice."

Neither Namath nor the prisoner got any applause for his performance that morning, but Namath did on a number of other occasions. One occurred on September 24, 1972, when he passed for almost 500 yards against the Baltimore Colts.

That performance by Namath, in a shoot-out with Johnny Unitas, is 1 of 12 individual and team achievements saluted in the following pages as Hallmarks of Excellence. Included are Namath's 496 yards passing, Walter Payton's 275 yards rushing, Tom Dempsey's 63-yard field goal, Miami's perfect season, and more—all of which are targets for those who play in the eighties to shoot at.

Gale Sayers Scores Six Touchdowns

December 12, 1965

George Halas, of the Chicago Bears, had spent a considerable amount of time debating in his own mind whether to risk a first-round draft choice on the kid from Kansas. The way Halas saw it, Gale Sayers had a lot going for him, but "we thought some of his performance was just luck." Then, just before the draft, Halas saw a reel of film that was all the convincing he needed. "I saw a highlight film on him, where he made two moves in one stride and ran ninety-five yards," Halas remembers. "That was it."

Halas, of course, turned out to be right. But even he was amazed by the performances Sayers turned in during his rookie season, particularly the one-man show he put on at Chicago's rain-soaked Wrigley Field, December 12, 1965.

In all the games ever played in NFL history, only three players ever have managed to score six touchdowns in one game. Ernie Nevers of the Chicago Cardinals did it in 1929, Dub Jones of the Cleveland Browns did it in 1951, and Sayers did it that damp December day.

Sayers, however, was the only player to achieve what is one of the rarest feats in the record books in the post-1960 period, during which NFL defenses gained recognition for their exceptional ability. No player since then has even been able to score as many as five touchdowns in a single game. This makes Sayers' achievement one of the targets to shoot at for every outstanding running back parading his talents in the NFL during the eighties.

Ironically, all three six-touchdown games involved the Bears, Nevers and Jones having reached the plateau in games against Halas' team. Sayers turned the tables in leading the Bears to a 61–20 romp over the San Francisco 49ers.

The 22-year-old Kansas comet got himself rolling with an 80-yard run after taking a screen pass from Rudy Bukich. Then Sayers tacked on four rushing touchdowns—a 21-yard sweep, a 7-yard sweep, a 50-yard sprint with a pitchout, and a 1-yard dive. And, finally, he topped it all off with a magnificent 85-yard punt return that displayed all his assets—speed, balance, direction change.

Preceding pages: Miami's Jim Kiick (21) runs for a touchdown in Super Bowl VII. Opposite: In a 1979 AFC playoff game, Houston's Vernon Perry intercepted a record four times in a game.

The first five times Sayers scored there was little outward display of emotion. He simply handed the ball to the official and jogged to the sidelines. But after the record-tying punt return, Sayers flipped the ball into the air, clapped his hands together, danced a few steps, and then ran to the bench where he was hoisted into the air by a number of his teammates.

In all, Sayers had gained 326 yards rushing, receiving, and returning while bringing his touchdown total to a season record 22 (surpassed in 1975 when O. J. Simpson scored 23).

"It was," Halas remembers, "the greatest performance I've ever seen on the football field by one man." So great, it's conceivable that Sayers might have even surpassed Nevers and Jones if the circumstances had been different. "That mud affected the kid," tight end Mike Ditka pointed out at the time. "If it had been dry out there, he would have scored ten touchdowns."

Six, however, seemed enough to impress everyone on both sides. "He has the three things that a good back must have," said Jon Arnett, a star with the Bears for eight seasons who had been beaten out by Sayers. "He has the ability to change directions, he has balance, and he has speed. A lot of guys in this league get by on just two of those. And he's tough. A lot of guys can't take it, but he can. That's what veterans look for in a rookie—to see if they're tough. He is."

"I wish I had the vocabulary to describe Sayers," said John David Crow, a 1,000-yard ground gainer for the 49ers. "He's a great, great football player already at a very young age. He's got quickness and speed—obviously—but he has something else a great back must have. He has a sense of football, a feel for the game."

"Sayers is the greatest runner I've ever seen," said El Kimbrough, the veteran San Francisco defensive back. "And that includes Jimmy Brown."

Meanwhile, in the Chicago dressing room, the shy and reticent Sayers was trying to elude that comparison just as he had eluded tacklers on the field. But he wasn't having as much success with the writers as he had had with the 49ers.

"I'm not any Jimmy Brown, I'll tell you that," he said in protest to those pushing the comparison. "Brown just does a whole lot of things that I can't do. He's the most exciting player I've ever seen. For one thing, I can improve upon my blocking. There are other things, too. A rookie has a lot of things he can improve upon."

And Gale Sayers improved upon them all dur-

ing a career that saw him elected to the Hall of Fame. But, despite the fact he played through the 1971 season before injuries struck him down, he never did score six touchdowns again.

But then neither has anyone else.

Tom Dempsey Kicks 63-yard Field Goal
November 8, 1970

Defensive tackle Alex Karras really put it in perspective after his Detroit Lions had been beaten by the New Orleans Saints. "When you put the ball down on the thirty-seven-yard line," he said, "you should kick it toward the nearest goal post, not the farthest."

Common sense might tell you that, but that's not what the Saints did on November 8, 1970, when they trailed the Lions 17–16 with two seconds to go. The ball was placed down on the 37-yard line—but placekicker Tom Dempsey was facing the farthest goal post.

The longest field goal in NFL history until then had been the 56-yarder kicked by Bert Rechichar of the Baltimore Colts in 1953. No one in 17 years had approached the record; no one had ever tried a field goal from 63 yards away. And certainly not a placekicker with Dempsey's handicaps—he was born without a right hand and with only a stump on his right kicking foot.

Yet J. D. Roberts, making a mid-season debut as the Saints' coach, immediately called on Dempsey for the record-breaker. "I looked at Tom," said Roberts, "and told him, 'Give it your best shot.' He nodded and replied, 'I'm ready coach.' "

And he was. For Tom Dempsey slammed the stump of his right foot into the ball held by Joe Scarpati and it soared through the goal posts 63 yards away, giving the Saints a 19–17 win and Dempsey a spot in the record book. Dempsey still holds that spot in the record book and his 63-yarder is obviously the prime target for any field goal kicker in the 1980s.

But giving Dempsey a spot in the record book hardly seemed enough at the time given the incredible difference between his field goal and Rechichar's, the seven yards representing an amazing 15 percent increase.

The Lions were, of course, stunned by what happened. "Unbelievable," said the Lions' placekicker, Errol Mann. "A miracle," said linebacker Mike Lucci. "It's hard to understand," said linebacker Wayne Walker, adding, "it's a miracle. Bobby Thomson's home run . . . nothing compares to it."

Tom Dempsey made it all happen because of the belief that he wasn't handicapped despite his handicaps, a belief that was instilled in him by his parents. "I'll always be thankful for my parents' attitude toward me when I was a small boy," Dempsey emphasizes. "They wouldn't let me feel sorry for myself because I was born with only half my right foot and no right hand. They taught me to get out and compete, and earn my place in life. I have to admit that the handicap is there; then I say I'm not handicapped—I can do anything anyone else can do."

He got his chance to prove he could do something no one else could after Mann had put the Lions out front with an 18-yard field goal, capping an 86-yard drive in 17 plays and leaving only 18 seconds remaining. The Lions' kickoff was taken by Al Dodd, who sped 14 yards to New Orleans' 28 before stepping out of bounds with eight seconds on the clock. Dodd then got it into range for Dempsey, grabbing a 17-yard pass from Billy Kilmer and stepping out of bounds again.

Roberts and Dempsey exchanged their few words, then Dempsey and Scarpati trotted onto the field for the attempt. "When we got into the huddle," Scarpati revealed, "I asked the guys up front to hold them [the Lions] just a little longer than usual. Then, when we were setting up, I told Tom that I was back a little deeper so that he would have an instant longer."

As a rule, field goals are attempted from seven yards behind the line of scrimmage. Scarpati was setting up eight yards back. Neither that, nor the noise beginning to build from the 66,910 fans inside Tulane Stadium, bothered Dempsey.

"I knew I could kick it sixty-three yards," he said, "but I wasn't sure that I could kick it straight. I got a good snap and a perfect hold. Naturally, I felt the pressure. But all that I was thinking about was kicking it as hard as I could."

Dempsey never did see the ball clear the crossbar. "I couldn't follow it that far," he said, "but I did see the [officials'] arms go up." When they went up, so did Dempsey and Roberts, on the shoulders of teammates who immediately paraded them around the field.

But it wasn't until several days later that Dempsey fully realized what he had achieved.

"Right at the time, I didn't realize what I had done," Dempsey explained. "I didn't go out to kick a sixty-three-yard field goal. I went out to win the game, and when I did, I was pretty happy. Everybody was. We went out that night and tied one on pretty good. It was a couple of days before the record hit me. I was sitting in the dressing room and I looked at a football and said, 'Damn, that thing went sixty-three yards.'"

Dolphins-Chiefs Play Longest Game
December 25, 1971

Garo Yepremian, the balding Cypriot who did the placekicking for the Miami Dolphins during their Super Bowl seasons, arrived in Kansas City with a chip on his shoulder. And it had nothing to do with the fact the Dolphins would be playing on Christmas Day. "I had found out [the day before] there would be no trip to the Pro Bowl for me," Yepremian explained at the time. "I came to Kansas City determined to show them I'm a good kicker."

Yepremian wasn't about to admit it, but his usually pleasant disposition wasn't helped by the fact that, while he had not been chosen for the Pro Bowl, the honor *had* been accorded to the Chiefs' Norwegian-born boomer, Jan Stenerud. And, while this AFC playoff game played on Christmas Day, 1971, had nothing really to do with the personal duel between Yepremian and Stenerud for supremacy among immigrant placekickers, it would ultimately be decided by the outcome of their confrontation.

The game, however, rests in the record books on the merits of its singular stature as "the Longest Game"—a slugging match between two obviously evenly matched teams that didn't end until 82 minutes and 40 seconds had elapsed.

Then, and only then, with night beginning to fall on Kansas City's Municipal Stadium, Yepremian stepped center stage with an opportunity to thumb his nose at those who had overlooked him for the Pro Bowl and kicked a 37-yard field goal that gave Miami a 27–24 win.

No game since has come close to matching that length of time and few have matched its intensity. And, oddly interwoven, was the personal battle between Yepremian and Stenerud. Stenerud kicked a first-quarter field goal, but Yepremian matched that in the second period and each team scored a touchdown for a 10–10 halftime tie. Each team scored two touchdowns in the second half, the Dolphins tying it with 1:36 left in regulation on a five-yard pass from Bob Griese to Marv Fleming.

Stenerud then had two chances to win it before Yepremian did. Ed Podolak, who gained 350 yards rushing, receiving, and kick returning in an outstanding performance that often is overlooked, took the kickoff following the Miami touchdown and raced 78 yards to the Miami 22. But, with 31 seconds left, Stenerud sent his 31-yard field goal attempt wide to the right. In overtime, the Chiefs won the toss, took the kickoff, and marched downfield to the Miami 35, where Stenerud tried a 42-yarder. This time, however, the snap was slightly high and Dolphins' linebacker Nick Buoniconti burst through to block the kick. In the only other scoring opportunity in the first overtime, Yepremian attempted a 52-yard field goal. He missed too.

The slugging match continued into the second overtime with the Dolphins gaining possession at their own 30 after three minutes. For the next five plays, Jim Kiick and Larry Csonka, the Dolphins' one-two punch, took turns carrying the ball.

Kiick and Csonka had been contained up until that point but, after Kiick started the winning drive with a 5-yard gain, Csonka ripped off the most important yardage of the game, darting through the left side and rambling 29 yards to the Kansas City 36 before he was brought down.

The Dolphins hadn't used the play on which Csonka broke loose all day, but Griese decided that play was the best one remaining in the Dolphins' arsenal. There also was another simple reason for his choice—he had used everything else. "The game was so long," Griese explained, "we'd used all our plays, so we thought we'd try it. Csonka likes to run it, so we used it."

On the sidelines, Yepremian sensed he was going to get another chance to win the game. "I thought when we were driving I could make anything under fifty yards," Yepremian said. "On the sideline, I was dying to get a chance to kick it."

Kiick, Csonka, and Kiick slammed into the line, in that order, on the next three plays, gaining six yards and positioning Yepremian for a 37-yarder. "There was a lot of pressure," Yepremian said, "but I tried to put it out of my mind."

Mike Kolen snapped the ball, Karl Noonan placed it down, and Yepremian swung his foot through in a high arc. "I had a good follow through," Yepremian recalled. "When you do that,

you get the ball up and there's less chance for anybody to block it. After I kicked the ball [and it went through the uprights], I looked up at the sky and thanked God for giving me the chance to kick it."

The Dolphins, of course, were delirious. The Chiefs were crushed, particularly Stenerud. "As I walked toward the locker room, I didn't want to have anything to do with this game again," Stenerud said in recalling his feelings several days after the game. "I was supposed to play in the Pro Bowl but I didn't know for a while whether I would play in that game."

He did. Yepremian didn't.

Joe Namath Passes for 496 Yards
September 24, 1972

Deep in the catacombs of Baltimore's Memorial Stadium, Johnny Unitas was surrounded by members of the press, which wasn't unusual. But they weren't there to talk about Unitas, which was unusual. This day they were there to talk about Joe Namath of the New York Jets and his ability to pass against a zone defense.

"That Namath," Unitas said with a wry smile on his lips, "he doesn't know any better than to put the ball up for grabs, throwing it deep against a zone defense." Unitas was, of course, being facetious, and everyone knew it, because he had just come off the field after going head-to-head with Namath in one of the most brilliant passing duels in NFL history.

The legendary Unitas completed 26 of 45 attempts for 376 yards and two touchdowns, but he hadn't even come close to Namath's totals. Namath tried just 28 passes and hit on only 15, but shredded the Colts' defense for an eye-opening 496 yards and six touchdowns in the most dazzling show of long-distance passing since the zone had been perfected.

Norm Van Brocklin of the Los Angeles Rams had passed for 554 yards in 1951 and Y. A. Tittle of the New York Giants had passed for 505 yards in 1962, but no one had been able to come close to 500 again once the zone became the standard pass defense for most teams. Even today, in the era of liberalized rules favoring passing, Namath's performance on that September 24, 1972, has not been approached, making it one of the most coveted targets for quarterbacks hoping to make their marks in the pass-conscious decade of the eighties.

There is no better description of what happened that day on the turf of Memorial Stadium before a crowd of 56,626 than the words uttered by Baltimore coach Don McCafferty in his office following the shoot-out. "It was discouraging," said an incredulous McCafferty. "We'd put together a good drive and score a touchdown to get back in the game and then Namath would score with one swing of his arm."

Appearing for the first time before the fans who had worshiped Unitas for so many seasons, Namath showed them why he now wore the crown. He threw for touchdowns of 80, 79, and 10 yards to Rich Caster, 67 yards to John Riggins, 65 yards to Ed Bell, and 21 yards to Don Maynard. And the experts were still arguing long after the game was over whether Namath was more brilliant at the end of the first half, when he connected for three touchdowns in a period of 1:29, or in the fourth quarter, when he connected with Caster for the 79- and 80-yarders on consecutive plays.

Even Namath's teammates marveled at his performance, particularly linebacker Al Atkinson. "What he did in beating them in the Super Bowl [the Jets beat the Colts, 16–7, in Super Bowl III] was fantastic," said Atkinson, "but those two first-down passes [to Caster], and his throwing in this one, are something I'd never have believed possible."

Namath looked for Caster the first time midway through the fourth quarter, after the Colts had pulled to within 3, 30–27. On the first play from scrimmage after the kickoff, Namath went deep downfield for Caster on a 79-yard play.

It had taken the Colts 14 plays to score their touchdown, while just one play enabled Namath to get the score back. But Unitas pulled the Colts together for still another drive, this one taking 11 plays before a touchdown was put up on the scoreboard. After the ensuing kickoff, Namath went back to Caster on the first play, this time for 80 yards. That was the final discouraging blow for the Colts. There was no way to recover from that.

After it was all over, after all the passes had been completed, Namath stood in the Jets' dressing room, slipping an elaborate brace off his left leg and trying to determine whether this had, indeed, been the best day of his celebrated career.

"I didn't think I threw the ball that sharp," Namath said. "I know it sounds dumb, but I've had better days throwing the ball. Sometimes I threw it short. Sometimes I was long. And sometimes where

I wanted to be. The last touchdown to Caster was a well-thrown ball, but the rest didn't feel so well thrown to me. It's like, did you ever hit a home run but when you hit the ball you didn't think you'd hit it well enough to make it go out? That's what it was like."

Still, Namath had to admit neither he nor many other passers had managed to put together six-touchdown days. "I don't think I've ever thrown that many in one game before," he said. "But if I have, it was way back on Sixth Street in Beaver Falls."

Namath's hometown is Beaver Falls, Pennsylvania, and Sixth Street was the scene of some of his best passing performances. Baltimore's Memorial Stadium was the scene of *the* best.

Franco Harris Makes Immaculate Reception
December 23, 1972

Twenty-two seconds remain. The Oakland Raiders lead the Pittsburgh Steelers 7–6 in a first-round AFC playoff game. The Steelers have the ball, but they face a fourth-down-and-10 situation from their own 40-yard line.

Pittsburgh coach Chuck Noll sends in a play from the sidelines with rookie receiver Barry Pearson. It turns out Pearson is carrying in a play designating himself as the primary receiver. In the huddle, quarterback Terry Bradshaw calls it.

Bradshaw takes the snap from center, fades back, is forced out of the pocket by the Raiders' fierce pass rush, desperately looks for Pearson, and then, as he is about to disappear in a sea of silver and black, launches a pass that flutters downfield. The ball seems to hang in the cold winter air for anyone to grab, but it winds up taking what many will later consider to have been a predestined route.

The route brings the ball into an area occupied by both Oakland safety John Tatum and Pittsburgh running back John ("Frenchy") Fuqua, who converge and leap for the ball at the same time at the same spot. The ball hits someone—either one or both of the players—and arches backward seven yards. Trailing the play, running back Franco Harris of the Steelers races toward the rebounding ball, reaches down to grab it before it hits the ground at the Oakland 42, and races virtually untouched into the end zone for an apparent touchdown.

What everyone had just witnessed would eventually be labeled the Immaculate Reception, but at the moment no one thought in those terms. They only wondered out loud what really happened, whether they had actually seen what they believed they had seen.

Referee Fred Swearingen decided to get at least one opinion to verify his and proceeded to use a dugout telephone to confer with Art McNally, the NFL supervisor of officials who had been seated in the press box with a television monitor by his side.

McNally: "How do you rule?"

Swearingen: "Touchdown."

McNally: "That's right."

With that, the touchdown was signaled and the Steelers were 13–7 winners. The single most unique play in NFL history had transformed an interesting but hardly spectacular playoff into the game voted the most memorable of the 1970s. It is the game by which all those played in the 1980s will be measured for their ability to stir memories. And there's no doubt that the "game of the Immaculate Reception" still does that—primarily because, to this day, what happened two days before Christmas, 1972, still seems so incredible.

It certainly was to those who had just been witnesses.

"I've been playing football since the second grade and I've never seen anything like this," Bradshaw said at the time.

"I can't believe it," said Pittsburgh guard Bruce Van Dyke. "I saw it, and I can't believe it. My damn brain is gone."

"I was talking to the man upstairs, so I didn't see the play," said Steeler defensive end L. C. Greenwood. "I didn't want to interrupt what I was doing. Next thing I know, the guys are jumping around and there goes Franco and I'm saying, 'Lord, I hope he has the ball.' "

"It's enough," said Harris, "to make you believe in God, if you didn't already. After today, I believe in Santa Claus too."

Controversy, however, still surrounds the play. Under the rules at that time, if the ball had struck Fuqua instead of Tatum, Harris' reception would have been ruled an incomplete pass. Tatum still insists that's what happened. "All I was trying to do was knock the ball loose," he says. "I touched the man [Fuqua] but not the ball. It hit Frenchy, and he knows it."

Steeler Franco Harris (32) runs with his "Immaculate Reception." Oakland led the 1972 playoff game, 7–6, with 22 seconds left. Bradshaw's pass was hit from Fuqua's hands into Franco's.

Fuqua declines to be drawn into any lengthy discussion of the subject. "I put the answer in a time capsule," he offers.

Bradshaw and Harris, meanwhile, profess ignorance. "I wasn't supposed to be there," says Harris. "I saw Terry throw and I started running to block if Frenchy caught the ball."

"I got knocked down [and didn't see it]," Bradshaw explains.

And Noll, who sent in the original play, will only give this play-by-play recitation without any elaboration: "Pearson got hung up and Frenchy adjusted his route and Terry went to him. Tatum hit the ball and Franco made a fantastic catch. Franco had been blocking on the play and then went out. He was hustling . . . and all good things happen to those who keep hustling."

So much for getting a better perspective on history.

Dolphins Wrap Up Perfect Season

January 14, 1973

Even then, on the day the Miami Dolphins made history by completing the only perfect season in NFL history with a 17–0 record, Larry Csonka felt compelled to speak about the Dolphins' place in history.

"Do you think people will give us credit now for what we've done?" Csonka asked after the Dolphins had whipped the Washington Redskins, 14–7, in Super Bowl VII. "If we were the New York Jets or the Los Angeles Rams we'd get recognized as a pretty good football team. But the critics have low rated us all season.

"They said we had a soft schedule. Did we make the schedule? Besides, some of the teams we beat knocked over clubs that made it into the playoffs. The only thing we failed to do this season is get the kind of publicity the big metropolitan teams usually rate. We're the best. We've just won the Super Bowl. Will someone please write something other than we're a bunch of nobodies?"

Someone may have, but obviously not too many. The 1972 Miami Dolphins—the only NFL team in history ever to make it through the regular season and postseason without losing a game—have never been fully honored for their unprecedented achievement.

No team from the NFL's inception in 1920 until the Dolphins in 1972 was able to make it through the NFL schedule without losing a single game, and no team since then has been able to duplicate the feat. Yet there wasn't that much fanfare at the time, and there certainly hasn't been that much since. Maybe it's the fact that the Super Bowl score doesn't indicate how the Dolphins dominated the Redskins. Maybe it's the fact that domination made for a dull game.

Whatever the reasons, the fact is that the Dolphins' achievement remains singular and has to be considered one of the two major targets for any team seeking a place in NFL history during the decade of the eighties. Because when it comes to unmatched team achievements, there are two standards—the four Super Bowls won by the Pittsburgh Steelers during the seventies and the perfect season fashioned by Don Shula's Dolphins in 1972.

It isn't often remembered, but the Dolphins put together their unblemished record in an unusual fashion, starting the season with Bob Griese at quarterback before going to Earl Morrall in the fifth game when Griese broke his ankle. Morrall gave way to the returning Griese midway in the AFC championship game victory over Pittsburgh. Griese was at the controls of the run-oriented Miami offense revolving around Larry Csonka and Jim Kiick for Super Sunday, January 14, 1973.

The Dolphins actually put the game away in the first half when Griese passed 28 yards to Howard Twilley for one touchdown and Kiick barrelled a yard for another touchdown while the Dolphins' defense completely shut down the Redskins. The defensive unit, led by tackle Manny Fernandez, middle linebacker Nick Buoniconti, and safety Jake Scott, permitted Washington to cross midfield only once in the half.

It remained 14–0 until midway during the final quarter. Then a fluke play enabled the Redskins to make the score respectable, blunt the feeling of Miami's total domination, and, quite possibly, cost the Dolphins the adulation they might otherwise have received.

The Washington touchdown came after Miami placekicker Garo Yepremian tried to throw a pass following a muffed field goal attempt. His wobbly pass was intercepted by Mike Bass, who raced 49 yards for the score, thus narrowing the margin to 14–7.

The final score doesn't even hint at the disparity between the two teams. It has to be pointed out that not only was a shutout lost because of Garo's

47

goof, but the Dolphins also had a 55-yard TD pass from Griese to Paul Warfield nullified by a penalty and two other drives halted by penalties.

In the Miami dressing room, Fleming and Buoniconti both took time to try to put the game, the season, and the Dolphins' place in the record book into perspective. "This team is better than the championship ones I was on with Green Bay," said Fleming, who played for Lombardi's Super Bowl winners. "We worked to win in Green Bay. We play to win in Miami. This team has more of a will to win. That's the difference. That's why we're better. That's why we're the best ever."

"We're as good as you guys make us," Buoniconti said, addressing the press in much the same manner as Csonka. "If you say we're the greatest team of all time, then we'll be rated the greatest. But one thing no one will ever be able to take away from us is our seventeen and 0 record. We're the only NFL team ever to do that. And we'll probably be the only team that ever does it."

He could very well be right.

O. J. Simpson Rushes for 273 Yards

November 25, 1976

It was Thanksgiving Day, 1976, and throughout the land turkeys were in ovens and football fans were in front of television sets. The traditional game in Detroit matched the Lions, with the NFL's top-ranked defense, against the woeful Buffalo Bills, who had lost seven consecutive games.

It didn't figure to be much of a contest, and it wasn't. The Lions won handily, 27–14, in a game that wasn't as close as the score indicated. But anyone who turned off his TV set early missed the greatest one-man show of running the ball from scrimmage in NFL history as O. J. Simpson careened for 273 yards in 29 carries. (A year later, Walter Payton of the Chicago Bears gained 275 yards, but it took Payton 40 carries to eclipse Simpson's mark.)

For many, it was the last opportunity to see one of the Juice's great performances—the 1976 season was the last in which he was able to gain 200 yards in a single game and the last in which he reached the 1,000-yard mark. Injuries would slow the Bills' great running back and force his retirement. But this Thanksgiving Day, in his ninth sea-

son, O. J. Simpson was at his best, sprinting outside and barrelling inside against the determined Detroit defense.

The crowd of 66,875 in the Pontiac Silverdome roared its approval of the Lions when they stopped O. J. for no gain on his second carry, then roared even louder in the final quarter as he made his run at the record.

Simpson entered the fourth quarter with 181 yards and the Bills trailing, 27–7, the lone Buffalo score coming on a 48-yard touchdown jaunt by O. J. that was his longest run of the day. With the game out of reach, Bills' coach Jim Ringo gave quarterback Gary Marangi the green light to showcase Simpson—and the quarterback proceeded to do exactly that.

Marangi handed Simpson the ball six consecutive times. On the sixth, he ran left behind guard Joe DeLamielleure and bolted 16 yards to the Detroit 15. The record was his—he had reached 261 yards, surpassing the 250 he had gained against the New England Patriots in 1973.

As the scoreboard lit up with the information, the crowd rose for a standing ovation and O. J. trotted over to the sidelines and embraced Ringo, the architect of the offensive line which had paved the way for Simpson's record-breaking feats. He then shook hands with teammates as the stadium rocked with chants of "Juice, Juice, Juice."

O. J. stayed in the game and watched Marangi hand off to Jeff Kinney, who lost two yards. Then Marangi went back to pass three consecutive downs, firing incomplete to Bob Chandler each time. But, on the last play, the Lions were offside and the Bills had one more chance.

This time Marangi called for a draw with Simpson carrying and the Juice dashed straight up the middle for 12 yards and a touchdown that put the final flourish on his exceptional performance. The drive had covered 58 yards, and O. J. had gained every one of those yards in seven carries.

But O. J. collected more than the single-game rushing record against the Lions. The 273-yard day was the fifth 200-yarder of his career—also an NFL record, which he later increased to six—and gave him a season total of 1,229 yards. It was the fifth time in his career, including his record 2,003-yard season in 1973, that he had exceeded the 1,000-yard mark. It also was his last.

But no one was aware of that at the time, and there was nothing but praise offered by the Lions. "There is only one O. J. Simpson," said Lions' coach Tommy Hudspeth. "He's one of a kind."

Even Detroit running back Dexter Bussey, who gained 137 yards rushing in a performance that normally would have made headlines locally, was awed by Simpson's amazing achievement. "I guess being on the same field with him psyched me up," Bussey said. "I always knew he was a great running back but he really made a believer out of me. He's like an antelope. He's graceful, he accelerates and shifts like no one I've ever seen."

O. J. was in his usual share-the-honors mood. "I'm very proud of the records and I'm very proud of our offensive line," he said. "Of course, the feeling is always better when you win. The day I had two-hundred fifty yards in a game we won. And the day I went over two thousand yards we won. What makes this game so satisfying, even though we lost, is that we knew we were coming into this stadium against the top defense in the league. This in itself was a challenge for me and for our offensive line. I am surprised we had the rushing yardage against them we did."

Walter Payton Rushes for 275 Yards

November 20, 1977

It was all over. Walter Payton had broken O. J. Simpson's single-game rushing record. Now he was standing in the Chicago Bears' dressing room under Soldier Field surrounded by reporters, being pressed to answer the question they had asked: How do you stop Walter Payton? For a moment, Payton didn't seem to have an answer, then he found one. "The night before a game," Payton said, "I would kidnap me."

Obviously kidnapping Payton had to be the only way to stop him; the flu certainly hadn't. Playing with the remnants of a flu that slammed into his body earlier in the week, Payton went out on November 20, 1977, and slammed through the Minnesota Vikings like a virus.

"I didn't think I could put on a Walter Payton performance when I left the dressing room [for the start of the game]," Payton said. "I had hot and cold flashes. And, I didn't feel good when I went out there for the introductions." Somewhere between the introductions and the first handoff Payton must have found a doctor with a miracle cure. The running back proceeded to carry on 40 of the

Bears' 71 offensive plays in a 10–7 victory.

And, when all the yardage was totaled up, Payton had shredded the Vikings' defense for 275 yards, breaking the single game record of 273 Simpson had established just a year earlier. It had taken Simpson 29 carries to amass almost the same total, but that didn't detract from Payton's performance. His workhorse role only seemed to enhance it. And, no matter how many carries it took, Payton's total is the standard for the best running backs of the eighties to try and surpass.

Admittedly, even Payton was surprised when the game was over and he was told he had carried so many times (one carry less than the all-time record held by Franco Harris of the Pittsburgh Steelers). "Forty?" Payton questioned. "It felt like about twenty. I didn't know it was that many. But I did have to 'suck it up' a little at times."

He had to suck it up because the Bears' game plan totally revolved around ball control—and ball control in this instance meant Payton. "We didn't go out to get Payton the yards," said quarterback Bob Avellini. "We just didn't want to do anything fancy, anything to hurt us. Walter can't hurt us."

"We swept right and left," said Payton. "I think we wore them down."

Payton certainly didn't wear down, pulling off his biggest gainer late in the fourth quarter with a 58-yard burst on his thirty-eighth carry. But, with time running down, Payton still was two yards short of the record at 271 after 39 carries. At this point, with the Bears on the six-yard line and a field goal easily in range, coach Jack Pardee decided to forego the kick in order to run more time off the clock. That gave Payton one more shot and he added four yards, enough to crack Simpson's record.

Pardee insisted after the game that he hadn't even known Payton was nearing Simpson's mark when he decided against the field goal. "Did Walter set a record?" Pardee asked. "I had no idea. I felt that [going for a field goal] was the only way we could lose, for them to block a kick and return it ninety yards for a touchdown like they did against Los Angeles last year."

Payton also said he wasn't aware he had a shot at any record until after it was announced that he had broken it. "I don't like people to come up and tell me during the course of a game," he explained. "It's something I don't like to hear."

In addition to breaking Simpson's coveted record, Payton broke the Bears' single-season record by bringing his total to 1,404 yards. He wound up the year with a 1,852-yard total that at the time was

the third best on the all-time list behind Simpson (2,003) and Jimmy Brown (1,863).

Payton also broke the Bears' one-game rushing record, held by Gale Sayers at 205 yards, and broke the team mark for carries he previously had established at 36. But, surprisingly, he scored only one touchdown, bulling one yard in the third period for the score that gave the Bears a tie before they won it on a Bob Thomas field goal.

There was, of course, the usual stream of superlatives spread around in the dressing rooms after the game. "There's no limit to what Payton can do," said Vikings' running back Chuck Foreman. "Payton was outstanding . . . the best back in football," said Vikings' coach Bud Grant. "He had a great day. This is his field, where he does his thing."

As a matter of fact, the least impressed person appeared to be Payton. "Maybe later it will mean something, in three or four years when I'm out of football," he said. "Right now, it's just another game."

Not to anyone who saw it.

Lynn Swann Sets Receiving Record

January 18, 1976

The five starters for Serra High School in Foster City, California, would trot out onto the court. The 5-foot 10½-inch guard named Lynn Swann would assume his post at center court for the opening tap. There had to be quite a few opposing centers who doubled over with laughter—until the ball was tossed up, and Swann leaped into the air and tapped it to a teammate. Swann may not have had the height to play center, but he did have the spring needed to control the opening tap.

"We had this jumping machine in high school," Swann pointed out, trying to place his leaping ability in focus. "Our coach had us go up and get balls. I could get up pretty well. How high is the rim, ten feet? I went up and got the ball at ten feet, three inches."

There are those who were in the Orange Bowl on January 18, 1976, for the playing of Super Bowl X who will swear Lynn Swann leaped even higher into the blue Miami sky to grab Terry Bradshaw's passes and lead the Pittsburgh Steelers to a 21–17 victory over the Dallas Cowboys.

Swann, still not fully recovered from a concussion just two weeks earlier, put on a fantastic display of his leaping ability in corralling four of Bradshaw's passes for 161 yards and the decisive touchdown on a 64-yarder.

Receivers have caught more passes in the Super Bowl, but not one has amassed as much yardage, making Swann's 161-yard total one of the best receiving performances in NFL history and a major target for the exceptional pass catchers of the 1980s.

Three of Swann's catches went for 149 of those yards, and bordered on the unbelievable. The first was a 32-yarder in the opening period that enabled Pittsburgh to continue a touchdown drive and tie the score, 7–7. Swann broke outside, recoiled from Mark Washington's one legal bump, turned up field, and leaped for the catch at the sidelines.

"Swann turned his body into an S-curve to reach the ball," said Pittsburgh coach Chuck Noll, amazed by the performance of the receiver he saw every game. "I don't know how he did it and still managed to stay in bounds."

Swann went to work on Washington again in the second period, tapping a ball to himself that appeared to be sailing out of reach and pulling it in as he fell for a 53-yard gain. "Bad timing," Swann pointed out. "I leaped too soon. Otherwise I wouldn't have had to tip the ball before I caught it."

Washington had twice played him almost perfectly and Swann had two receptions. Washington was right on Swann again for his fourth catch in the fourth quarter, racing downfield step for step with the fluid receiver, who leaped at the five-yard line and hauled in Bradshaw's pass for a 64-yard touchdown. "He [Washington] took the inside away from me," Swann explained. "I kept trying to get inside. He kept trying to keep me from it. So I just took it down the field. Terry saw me and got the ball to me."

The touchdown, with just 3:02 remaining, pulled the Steelers out front, 21–10, and proved to be the clincher when the Cowboys struck back for a second Roger Staubach touchdown pass shortly after.

The amazing thing is that Swann even played. Two weeks earlier a blow to the head had left him limp on a stretcher as he was carried from the field. The diagnosis was a concussion and there was considerable concern over whether Swann would—or even should—play in the Super Bowl.

"It was a lot like a kid falling off a horse,"

Swann said. "If you don't get back up right away, you might never ride again. I knew I had to play in the game. I had to prove it to myself. If a professional athlete kept dwelling on an injury, his career would be washed up. No one in my family objected to my playing. I've been hurt before. They knew this was an important game to me. But they also knew I felt no football game was worth risking my life to win. I was concerned about how I'd perform. I was all thumbs trying to catch the ball in practice this week. I guess laying off a while affected my concentration. Terry still had enough confidence to throw to me. And that first one [the 32-yarder] really picked me up."

Swann also played despite a week of verbal harassment from the Cowboys, who suggested Swann would be risking injury by playing against the hard-hitting Texans. "I read the papers," Swann admitted. "I saw what [safety] Cliff Harris was saying. What a hitter he was. How intimidated I'd be. And that if he was me coming off a concussion, he could understand why I would be intimidated. I said to myself, 'To hell with it. I am going out there and play a hundred percent.' That's what I did. It proved he [Harris] didn't know the Pittsburgh Steelers or me."

And may still not know him even now. It's tough to get to meet a guy who's usually 10 feet off the ground.

Terry Bradshaw Sets Super Bowl Records

January 21, 1979

"I'm not dumb," said Terry Bradshaw quietly, matter-of-factly, without rancor. "I never was dumb. Go ask Thomas Henderson if he thinks I'm dumb now."

And, with that, the quarterback for the Pittsburgh Steelers made sure he had had the last words in a verbal duel with the linebacker for the Dallas Cowboys that was the main event leading up to the playing of Super Bowl XIII. And also the last laugh.

Henderson thought he was getting that when, at the beginning of Super Bowl week, he suggested with a smirk that Bradshaw wasn't too sharp upstairs and underscored it by insisting the Pittsburgh passer couldn't spell *cat* if you spotted him the C and the A. Bradshaw never did prove he could spell

cat but he did prove he knew how to be an MVP.

Stung, very possibly by Henderson's tactless remarks, Bradshaw stepped into the Orange Bowl, January 21, 1979, and put together the best day he had ever had during his entire nine-year NFL career. What he did was completely riddle the Dallas defense for 17 completions in 30 attempts, establish Super Bowl records for passing yardage (318) and touchdown passes (4), and lead the Steelers to an unprecedented third Super Bowl victory.

Never before had Bradshaw been able to gain 300 yards or pass for four touchdowns in a single game—preseason, regular season, or postseason. Suddenly, he had accounted for the number-one passing performance in Super Bowl history—establishing the criteria by which all quarterbacks in the eighties will be judged.

Bradshaw opened the scoring with a 28-yard touchdown pass to John Stallworth. Then, after the Cowboys had taken a 14–7 lead, Bradshaw came back with a 75-yarder to Stallworth that tied the record for the longest in Super Bowl history. Before the half had ended—a half in which he surpassed the existing Super Bowl yardage record for an entire game—Bradshaw pulled the Steelers ahead 21–14 by finding Rocky Bleier with a seven-yarder.

Bradshaw closed out the Steelers' scoring with an 18-yard touchdown toss to Lynn Swann that made the score 35–17 and gave Pittsburgh the breathing room it needed to survive a frantic comeback led by Roger Staubach.

After the game, Bradshaw was smart enough to remember the details of every one of his touchdown passes: "The first was a play action to Stallworth, who made an inside move and then out to the end zone. He made a great catch. On the second one, Dallas tripled Swann. When I looked at Stallworth he was so wide open his first move, I didn't throw. But I did get it to him. He did a great job of running with the ball [after the catch]. The third one was an option run or pass. Rather than running for the first down, I saw Bleier making a good move and lofted it to him. Another good catch. The last one was the same as the first, a play-action pass, except it went to Swann."

But, if one touchdown was the turning point, it was a 22-yard bolt up the middle by Franco Harris after Dallas had inched to within 21–17—and that came right after Bradshaw and Henderson had an on-the-field confrontation in the Steelers' backfield.

On that play, Pittsburgh faced a third-and-four at the Dallas 17. Bradshaw took too much

Above: *Lynn Swann, spectacular wide receiver for the Pittsburgh Steelers, does his thing against a tenacious Baltimore defender.*
Opposite: *A familiar sight, Swann gliding toward the end zone.*

time to get off the play but, despite a whistle for a delay-of-game penalty, the ball was snapped and Henderson broke through and slammed Bradshaw to the ground. Harris didn't appreciate Henderson's act and told him so. Then he went back to the huddle, smiled when he heard Bradshaw call his number, and raced up the middle for a touchdown that boosted the Steelers' lead to 28–17.

The call obviously had taken advantage of Harris' emotions. "Franco was mad because of what Henderson did to me," Bradshaw explained. "When I called his number, he ran so hard and so fast . . . he would have run through a brick wall if he thought the brick would keep him out of the end zone."

In the Dallas dressing room, there was only unadorned praise for Bradshaw.

"Any other quarterback wouldn't have been able to do that against our defense," said defensive end Harvey Martin. "Without Bradshaw the Steelers would be nothing."

"They don't do anything different from any other teams," said safety Cliff Harris. "It was Bradshaw. They are a really good team, but Bradshaw made them great. He deserved MVP."

"That Bradshaw throws the ball twenty yards downfield like I'd throw a dart fifteen feet," said the Cowboys' other safety, Charlie Waters, before being asked to discuss the subject of Bradshaw's brain power just one more time. "Do I think Bradshaw has outgrown the not-too-bright tag?" he asked, then answered. "You judge a man on how many Super Bowls he's taken his team to. He's been in the league nine years and won three Super Bowls."

That, of course, was a record. And he would add number four just a year later.

Vernon Perry Intercepts Four Passes

December 29, 1979

There have, undoubtedly, been any number of exceptional defensive performances in the history of the NFL. The difficulty in singling out defensive players always exists, however, because there are no yardsticks to accurately measure one performance against another. But, on December 29, 1979, an obscure defensive back named Vernon Perry, playing with the Houston Oilers, put on a one-man defensive show in an AFC playoff game against the San Diego Chargers that unquestionably set some standards.

All Vernon Perry did was intercept four passes—he just missed a fifth—thrown by AFC passing leader Dan Fouts, block a field goal attempt, and set up 10 of Houston's points in a 17–10 win over the Chargers.

In the history of professional football, four passes have been intercepted in a single game during the regular season by just 15 players from (believe it or not) Sammy Baugh in 1943 to Willie Buchanon in 1978. But no one ever had been able to do it in a postseason game until Perry. And, while Perry's performance had experts thumbing through record books to check and double-check the fact that his performance was unique in postseason play, others more interested in personal details scurried around trying to find out who he was.

Those who checked the Houston press guide—usually a storehouse of personal information—were disappointed to find that Perry was so obscure the Oilers hadn't even included his picture or anything more than the barest biographical sketch. The reason was simple—not much was actually known about Perry, even by coach Bum Phillips, the man who had decided to sign the 6-foot 2-inch, 210-pound veteran of two Canadian Football League seasons.

The one link between Vernon Perry and total obscurity was Robert Brazile, the outstanding linebacker for the Oilers who had attended college at Jackson State with the hard-hitting safety. Brazile knew Perry wanted to play in the NFL.

"Robert said he could play," Phillips explained. "And right there you've got a live report and a heckuva recommendation. Robert's like that television commercial—when he talks, you listen. Why not take a look, I thought. We sent scout Joe Woolley to watch Perry against the Hamilton Tiger Cats in the CFL playoffs, and Perry was outstanding with two interceptions. We were glad to get him."

What they got was one of the great pranksters of our time. "He is one real character," says defensive end Elvin Bethea. "He's what you would call a prankster of the first order. The guy kills me. He's always hiding my keys and putting ice in parts of my underwear [translation: jockey shorts]."

They also got one real outstanding defensive back, a guy who had been cut by the Chicago Bears but had made the most of his two years in Canada. "The field in Canada is bigger and, with only three downs [to make ten yards], they throw a lot more," Perry explained. "It gave me room to work. I learned a lot up there. But I thought I'd accomplished all I could and I wanted to give the NFL a try."

"Playing in Canada was good for him," said defensive coordinator Ed Biles. "You can't coach experience. He gets his hands on the football—in practice and in games—more than anyone I've ever seen. He either catches them or knocks them down. He seems to have a knack for making things happen. Vernon is a great athlete and great athletes make the big plays. Against the Chargers he played the best game I've ever seen from a defensive back."

The Chargers bolted to a 7–0 lead the first time they got the ball and it appeared they would take a commanding lead in the second quarter when Mike Woods set up for a 25-yard field goal. But Perry stormed through, blocked it, picked the ball up, and raced 57 yards to the San Diego 28. That was the first time the Oilers had managed to pierce the Chargers' 50-yard line and it resulted in a 26-yard field goal by Toni Fritsch.

Just three plays later, Perry turned in his first interception, returning seven yards to the San Diego 38 and setting up Houston's first touchdown. That gave the Oilers 10 points at a time they admittedly were struggling.

Perry made his final two interceptions in the closing four minutes of the game, the last one at the Houston 27, as the Chargers tried to battle from behind following a 47-yard pass from Gifford Nielsen to Mike Renfro that gave the Oilers a 17–14 lead.

Did Perry think one interception was more important than any other? "They all felt good," he answered. "All we knew was that Fouts was a fine passer and they told us, 'Just stop him and we'll win.' That was what I was trying to do."

Guess no one told Perry he didn't have to do it all by himself.

Steelers Win Fourth Super Bowl
January 20, 1980

Terry Bradshaw didn't like the play—didn't like it before he tried it, didn't like it after he tried it. All week long, the Pittsburgh Steelers had practiced the play—"Sixty prevent, slot hook and go"—and it hadn't worked.

"You've got to have confidence in a play," Bradshaw said, explaining his reservation about the deep pass to John Stallworth. "I ran that about eight times in practice and hadn't hit it once."

Bradshaw may not have liked it, but Chuck Noll, the Steelers' coach, loved it. Noll believed that Bradshaw would be able to throw deep against Los Angeles in Super Bowl XIV because Bud Carson, the Rams' defensive coordinator, had once been a Steeler assistant. Carson knew the basis for Pittsburgh's medium-range passing game, so Noll devised six or seven new plays for the Super Bowl, including the deep pass to Stallworth that Bradshaw would just as soon have done without.

"The Rams play a tough, short-passing defense," said Noll. "We wanted to show the short pass and then go deep with the slot man. We called it in our first possession in the first half, but Terry overthrew [Lynn] Swann. Then we called it twice more, both on those big plays to Stallworth."

Those big plays to Stallworth came in the fourth quarter after the Rams had built a 19–17 lead. The first was a 73-yard touchdown pass from Bradshaw. The second was a 45-yard connection between the two that set up the Steelers' last touch-

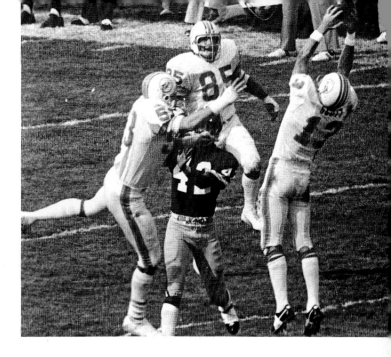

The Redskins' Charley Taylor (42) is surrounded by Miami defenders Scott (13), Buoniconti (85), and Matheson (53) in Super Bowl VII. Scott intercepted.

down. That was more than enough to enable the Steelers to whip the Rams, 31–19, and close out their domination of the seventies with their fourth Super Bowl victory in six years—twice as many as any other team had ever won.

Vince Lombardi's Green Bay Packers, Don Shula's Miami Dolphins, Tom Landry's Dallas Cowboys—they all had won two Super Bowls. Chuck Noll's Pittsburgh Steelers had doubled that, setting the standard by which all potential dynasties will be measured in the eighties.

Were the Steelers of the seventies actually a dynasty? Chuck Noll wasn't about to get caught patting himself on the back.

"Dynasty," he said when asked. "Is that a place to eat?"

What about it, Terry?

"I'd never say the Steelers are a dynasty," the quarterback replied.

Okay, then, Terry, what would it take for a team to be considered a dynasty?

Grinning, Bradshaw replied, "Probably winning four Super Bowls in six years."

Chuck Noll and Terry Bradshaw may not want to congratulate themselves for being the main men of a dynasty, but history will not have to argue long to determine whether, indeed, they were or were not a dynasty.

By any definition, they were. And, while Noll and Bradshaw wouldn't say so, cornerback Mel Blount was blunt about it. "I think winning this fourth Super Bowl should put us in a special category," he said. "I think this is probably the best team ever assembled. They talk about the Vince Lombardi era, but I think the Chuck Noll era is even greater."

There was an unusual amount of praise for the taciturn Noll, who despite the fact he had guided the Steelers to an unprecedented four Super Bowl wins, never had been accorded the honor of being selected coach of the year. "Charles Henry Noll is the guy who keeps it going," said defensive tackle Joe Greene. "He's the man that does it all."

But it wasn't easy on January 20, 1980. The Rams, who won the NFC championship with only a 9–7 record and came into the game with a quarterback—Vince Ferragamo—who had started only eight previous games, gave the Steelers all they could handle. "This," said Noll, "was probably the most physical Super Bowl game we've ever played. The Rams played well. They wanted it badly. They gave us a lot of problems, especially on offense. The difference in the game was our big plays."

Bradshaw, who admitted he "felt more pressure than in our other Super Bowls," did not have a particularly good day overall. He completed 14 of 21 passes for 309 yards, but three were intercepted and through three quarters Ferragamo was the hero, not Bradshaw.

Then Noll called the play Bradshaw didn't really want to try, and he connected with Stallworth for the 73-yarder. Later in the quarter, Bradshaw himself decided it was worth another shot, and Stallworth hauled another pass in.

The Steelers had done it again. And, if you believe safety J. T. Thomas, no one will ever be able to do what the Steelers did—achieve so much in so few years. "Before us there were none," said Thomas. "After us there will be no more."

4

Ten for the Hall

More than several seasons ago, when Don Klosterman was general manager of the Houston Oilers, Charlie Lockhart walked up to the reception desk and asked to see him. Since Lockhart was a former player—the Oilers had been forced to give him his release after he had undergone shoulder surgery—Klosterman told the receptionist he would be pleased to chat with Lockhart.

Lockhart, however, wasn't just dropping in to chat. He believed the Oilers owed him some back pay and he was calling on Klosterman to collect. It wasn't long before the conversation grew heated and then, suddenly, Lockhart pulled a gun. Fortunately, Houston scout Tom Williams, who had been in the office during the discussion, grabbed Lockhart and disarmed him before any damage could be done. "That's why," said Klosterman, as soon as he had regained his composure, "you have to hire good scouts."

The Klosterman anecdote may be entertaining, but it's obvious that good scouts have other duties. Primary among them is finding the players who will do for the eighties what players like O. J. Simpson and Fran Tarkenton, Roger Staubach and Mean Joe Greene did for the seventies: create the excitement that is what the NFL really is all about.

Who will be the most exciting players of the eighties? Who are the players who will run or pass or block or tackle well enough to make themselves Hall of Fame candidates in this decade? On the pages that follow, the good scouts of the NFL have singled out 10 players who are expected to perform with enough flair and ability to be among the elite of the eighties.

Phil Simms

Quarterback, New York Giants

It would have been impossible for Phil Simms to have missed the reaction. All he had to do was pick up a newspaper or flick on his TV and there was the demeaning sequence in words or pictures: the New York Giants announce they are making Phil Simms of Morehead State their number-one choice in the 1979 college-player draft and the team's fans respond with a chorus of boos.

It didn't stop there. You would have thought the Giants had drafted the Unknown Soldier. For the next several days, football fans kept asking each other, "Who's Phil Simms?" It occurred so often that when Simms showed up at the club's training camp, his teammates already had nicknamed him "Phil Who?"

Phil Simms, however, didn't resent it. If he had been a Giants' fan, he might have booed too. "Like the average fan, I think I'd have the same reaction," he said. "I expected it. I didn't figure the people in New York had ever heard of me. Most of them had never heard of Morehead. After getting their hopes up for a number one, I figured they'd raise a little hell when I was it.

"Even the people back home were shocked when I was drafted in the first round. The next day, the Louisville papers were critical of the Giants. They as much as said I had no right being drafted that high. That hurt, because I really thought they knew me. I hope in the near future they all get to know me better."

They should. The way the Giants talk the only question about Phil Simms is whether he's going to be more like Terry Bradshaw or Bob Griese.

"I worked out Phil myself," says coach Ray Perkins, "and learned all I needed to know. His motion, his style is similar to Terry Bradshaw. Phil Simms has a rare combination of qualities that doesn't come along that often. He has size, strength, arm strength, accuracy, excellent motion, and high intelligence. At some point in time, he has the chance to be a great NFL quarterback."

"He's going to be a great quarterback," agrees offensive lineman Gordon Gravelle, who previously played with the Pittsburgh Steelers and Bradshaw. "He's cooler than Bradshaw was at the same age."

"His long suit," says chief scout Jerry Shay,

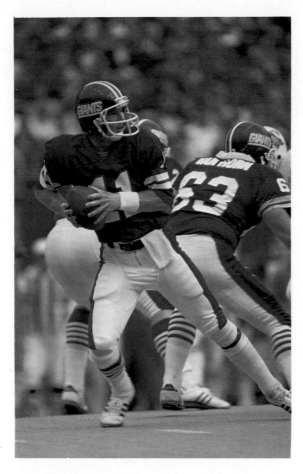

Above: *Phil Simms (11), first-round pick of the New York Giants in 1979, has the intelligence and abilities of quarterbacks like Griese and Bradshaw.* Right: *Billy Sims, Heisman trophy-winner from Oklahoma, ran for five touchdowns, rushed for 287 yards, and caught four passes in the first two games of his rookie season for the Detroit Lions.* Opposite: *Steve Largent (80), wide receiver for the Seattle Seahawks, whose disciplined and consistent patterns resulted in 71 receptions in 1978 and 1,237 yards gained in 1979.*

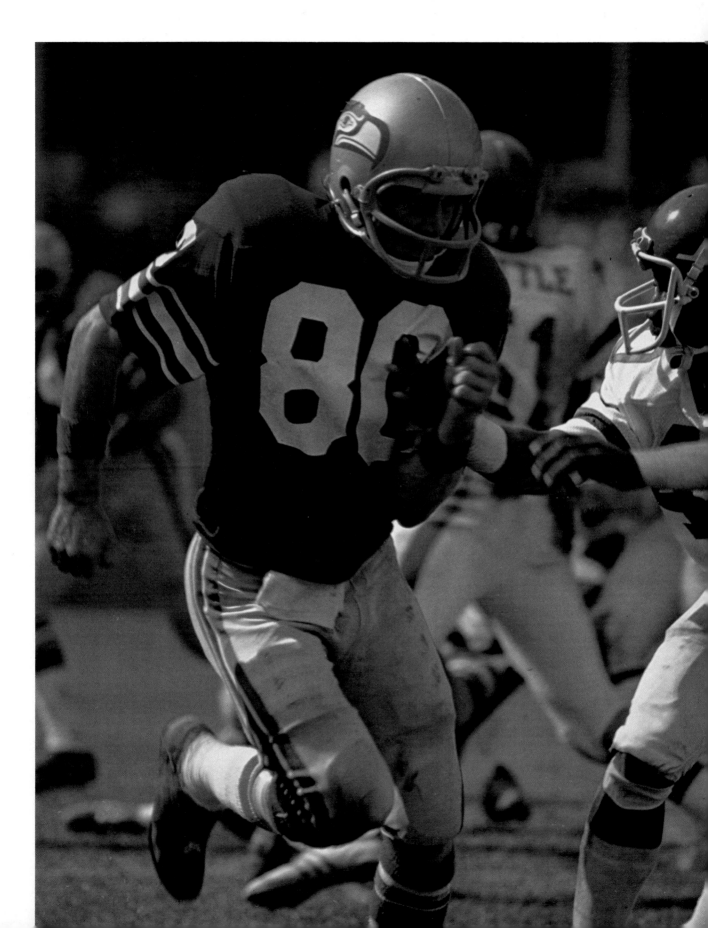

*Ozzie Newsome grabs a pass in a game against Miami. Cleveland's
first-round draft choice in 1978 was called "the best end in
Alabama history," by his college coach, Bear Bryant.*

"is he's a very intelligent kid. He has a lot of the intangibles a quarterback has to have. He has an accurate arm, can hit receivers at fifty yards and better. He has a good natural feeling for the passing game. He doesn't seem to get rattled under pressure.

"I played my college ball at Purdue, and Bob Griese was a year behind me. This kid has a lot of things Griese had. He's a quiet-type leader. He handles himself well and gives you confidence. I think the other players will look up to him that way."

So, who is Phil Simms and why was he such a mystery when he entered the NFL just before the curtain went up on the 1980s? The major reason Phil Simms was a mystery to the average fan was that he played his college ball at Morehead State, far from the major college spotlight that usually falls on quarterbacks from Alabama or Notre Dame or Southern California.

It also didn't help when Morehead State changed from a pro-set offense to the option in Simms's senior season. That resulted in a 3–8 record and considerable confusion about his ability, despite the fact he was the best quarterback in the school's history with 5,545 yards and 32 touchdowns.

But there were NFL teams who were able to read the situation as accurately as the Giants. It's no secret, points out Giants' general manager George Young, that 20 of the league's 28 teams made repeated trips to Kentucky—and it wasn't to watch the blue grass grow. "Do you think a lot of people were in a hurry to go to Morehead, Kentucky?" Young asks. "Is that the crossroads of the universe?"

Certainly not for the Giants. Their crossroads is East Rutherford, New Jersey, site of the stadium where Phil Simms, a 6-foot 3-inch, 215-pound quarterback with a Prince Valiant haircut, is expected to pull the perennial losers into title contention.

It is a challenge that Phil Simms is only too eager to take on. It is a challenge he was ready to take on even before people began to question who he was. He never needed that kind of motivation. "That didn't change anything," Simms says. "I already had the incentive. I wanted to play pro football, whether I was drafted in the first round or the tenth, whether the people booed me or greeted me with a marching band. I don't worry about proving anything to anybody but myself. The fans, they have one set of standards. The coaches have another. I have my own and they are the highest of

Opposite: *Houston's star running back Earl Campbell comes off the launching pad in a game against the Atlanta Falcons. After his 1978 rookie season, Campbell's phenomenal skills were recognized with 29 awards, including Rookie of the Year and MVP. "When you tackle him," says Washington linebacker Pete Wysocki, "it sure reduces your IQ." Above: Billy Sims shows Atlanta he's a dangerous receiver as well as a runner.*

all. If I can satisfy myself, I know I'll satisfy every-body else.

"Every quarterback in this league compares himself with every other one," Simms continues. "I know my limits, but I have absolute confidence in myself. I know, if I reach my potential, I'll be one of the best in the NFL. I know that, so I feel an obligation to go for it."

Earl Campbell

Running Back, Houston Oilers

There are a number of people who should know who insist that Earl Campbell is the nearest thing they've ever seen to Jimmy Brown. And that includes Jimmy Brown. "Earl Campbell," says Brown, "is the only player I like to look at. He reminds me of myself."

Jimmy Brown is, of course, the reigning NFL rushing record holder lifetime. But there's little doubt that he knows Earl Campbell will make a run at his record before the curtain goes down on the eighties.

Only two players in NFL history have ever gained more than 10,000 yards in their careers—Brown, with 12,312 yards in 9 seasons, and O. J. Simpson, with 11,236 in 11 years. Campbell got off to a faster start than either. He gained a rookie-record 1,450 yards—neither Brown nor Simpson surpassed 1,000 their first season—and headed into the 1980s at a pace which, if continued, would put him over the 12,000-yard mark during his eighth year.

But that's to be expected from the 5-foot 11-inch, 225-pounder who exploded onto the NFL scene in 1978 and immediately amassed 29 postseason awards, including MVP and Rookie of the Year, not to mention a collection of compliments that underscore his unique ability.

"I never played against Jim Brown," says defensive tackle Joe Greene of the Pittsburgh Steelers, "but he was always one of my favorites. But if Jim Brown was better than this guy, I wouldn't want to be around. He has strength, quickness, the ability to break tackles, and, above all, a tremendous determination. He may be even better than O. J. Simpson in that he can run right over you if he has to."

"When he hits that hole, it's like a door slamming," says Dwight White, another member of the Steelers' Front Four. "He's that brutal. He's more brutal than O. J. He's just a God-gifted athlete.

And he's young. He has that young body and that young enthusiasm."

"He runs," says Oakland coach Tom Flores, "like a freight train with agility."

"You can mention running backs and then you should mention Earl Campbell," says Ken Houston, the veteran Redskins safety. "He is in a class all by himself. It's next to impossible to bring him down. I hit him high in the Pro Bowl and he almost murdered me."

"His balance is unbelievable," says linebacker Greg Buttle of the New York Jets. "You hit him and he doesn't go down. He'll run into a pile, then everybody relaxes. When you look up, he's on his way downfield. How do you stop him? With a rifle."

"When you tackle him," says Washington linebacker Pete Wysocki, "it sure reduces your IQ."

"You watch him on film," says safety Tim Foley of the Miami Dolphins, "and you see him running over people and you think, 'He can't be that good. . . . Those guys must not be playing well.' Then after the game, you say, 'He's that good.' He's like O. J. Simpson in one sense. He does his talking with his running. You don't get a lot of lip from him. No show biz, just a lot of football."

It's this aspect of his character that Foley touches on which seems to impress almost everyone as much as Campbell's football ability. Just listen to center Carl Mauck of the Oilers: "His mother did a great job raising him. Heisman trophy and all, he came in here humbly and with a great attitude. As a person, he can't be beat."

And, what Mauck only guesses at, is true. His mother did a great job of raising him, but it wasn't easy. Fact is, Earl Campbell was known as "Bad Earl" when he was 1 of 11 Campbell children growing up in poverty in Tyler, Texas. And "Bad Earl" spent considerable time hanging around pool halls, drinking, smoking, and scuffling.

"I was lucky though," Campbell says with a grin. "Most of the places I went had back doors. When there weren't any, I could run fast enough not to get caught."

But when he's serious about the subject, he admits his mom got him straightened out. "I remember one thing my mother used to tell all of us," Campbell reveals. "She'd say to us, 'I love you. I'll try to feed you and I'll try to clothe you. But I won't spend any money to get you out of jail.'"

That message seemed to get across to Campbell, who went on to star at the University of Texas

Offensive guard Steve Courson (77) doubles up on the defender to spring Steeler teammate Franco Harris. Courson, at 6'1", 268 pounds, runs the 40 in under five seconds and can slam dunk a basketball.

Right: *Seahawks'
Steve Largent is
by himself at the
beginning of most
plays. As the
pattern develops,
however, he usu-
ally draws more
than one defend-
er.* Opposite:
*John Jefferson,
brilliant young
receiver for San
Diego, leaps for
another reception.*

before joining the Oilers and establishing a reputation for both his ability to run with the ball and his ability to handle himself.

Maybe it's because Earl Campbell is doing exactly what Earl Campbell has always wanted to do. Or, as he puts it, "You go to bed one night and dream of certain things. The next day you sit up and try to catch up with your dream. For so many years, all I've been doing is dreaming. I guess it's come true. I love playing football. I even enjoy practicing. It is a job, I guess, a way of making a living, like nine to five. But the hours are better, even if it's a little harder on Sundays and sometimes Monday."

Billy Sims

Running Back, Detroit Lions

The annual rookie initiation ceremonies at the Detroit Lions' training camp were well underway when Billy Sims stood up to introduce himself, staring straight into the audience of veterans. There was an expectant stir among those watching; Billy Sims was, after all, the most important rookie drafted by the Lions in several seasons—a running back with enough talent to command a $1 million bonus and a contract for another million.

"Hello," he said. "I'm Billy Sims from the University of Oklahoma. And I'm the reason most of you guys aren't getting raises this year."

Billy Sims paused and waited for the reaction. It was always possible that one or more of the veterans would fall off their chairs. It was certainly possible that one or more of the veterans would throw their chairs.

But Sims's introduction was taken in the spirit in which he had hoped it would be. "He broke us up with that line," recalls safety Jimmy Allen. "From then on life here has reminded me of the line Jackie Gleason used to open his show with, 'How sweet it is.' I mean I didn't know how good Billy Sims really was. Now I know he's for real.

"He's able to leap tall buildings at a single bound. He's Mr. Universe, except that he's short.

Mike Haynes (40), New England Patriots' cornerback, looks forward to passing games where receivers like the Jets' Jerome Barkum (83) try to invade his turf.

72

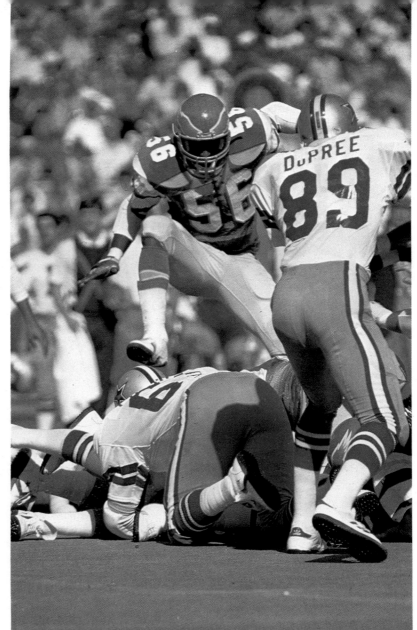

Left: *Chicago Bears' 6'5", 260-pound defensive end Dan Hampton (99) is nicknamed "Danimal" by his teammates. The unfortunate Detroit quarterback is about to receive a Hampton "hello."* Above: *Jerry Robinson (56), Eagles' tough linebacker, romps and stomps his way through the Dallas offense with 9.7 speed and bone-jarring pursuit.*

He's an incredible runner, but he's as strong as an offensive lineman. Television has a bionic man and we got our million-dollar man. And our guy is worth every cent of it. He's made the difference in our offense, but he's not selfish about it. He congratulates other players. If he thinks he's anything special, he keeps it to himself."

He may keep it to himself, but everyone knows—Billy Sims is, indeed, something special. It's not every day a running back enters the National Football League with his name already linked with O. J. Simpson, Earl Campbell, and the rest of the best.

And it's not every season that his teammates know after two games why a player's name is linked with the best. But the Lions did, just two games into Sims's 1980 rookie season. In those two games, both won by Detroit (matching the Lions' entire 1979 victory total), Billy Sims gained 287 yards for a 6.8 average, caught 4 passes for an additional 158 yards, and scored 5 touchdowns (no Lion scored more during 1979).

But Billy Sims was far from satisfied. "I still can get better," he said. "I have to get better." He said that because 100-yard days have been routine during his career. The challenge is in the 200-yarders. At Oklahoma, during his Heisman trophy-winning junior season, he put together three consecutive 200-yard games. And, as a senior, he accumulated 282 yards against Missouri.

"I believe those two-hundred-yard days will come—they always have," he says matter-of-factly because he does not indulge in boasting. "They have ever since I've been playing football. Even though the league is bigger and tougher now, those days are really possible."

That they are is amazing, for Sims is not overpowering—a 5-foot 11-inch, 208-pounder—and he really would have preferred to play basketball.

"I spent most of life wishing I was tall," he says, "but since it never worked out that way, I'm doing the best I can with what I have."

With what he has, Sims was nothing short of a sensation at Oklahoma, scoring 50 touchdowns, gaining more than two miles rushing, and fashioning a NCAA record career rushing average of 7.09 yards a carry. Sims already has made himself a millionaire with the Lions, thoroughly convinced his teammates of his ability, and set himself on a course many experts feel will eventually lead to the Hall of Fame.

And through it all, he has managed to maintain his equilibrium, showing no ego whatsoever

and giving every indication that he never will.

"My grandmother always told me never to forget where I was going," he explained, "where I came from, and the people who helped me along the way."

That's why Billy Sims began working with handicapped children during his days in Oklahoma. His brother, Dale, who died in June 1980, was mentally retarded. Billy Sims wants to devote his life to recreational therapy for the handicapped. Steps already have been taken to form a foundation in Billy Sims's name, specifically to raise money for handicapped children.

"So many families," Sims says, "are ashamed of their mentally retarded. They want to put them in a closet. Not me. I believe in miracles."

John Jefferson

Wide Receiver, San Diego Chargers

John Jefferson laughs when he tells the story about the vote for the number-one Texas schoolboy football player that occurred when he was in high school in Dallas, and he beat out the big running back from Tyler, Texas. "I had broken all the state's receiving records," Jefferson recalls. "I nudged Earl Campbell by one vote."

It is of more than passing interest to note that Jefferson and Campbell were not only just one vote apart in high school, but entered the NFL at the same time in 1978 and quickly established their Hall of Fame potential.

Campbell became the first rookie ever to win the league's rushing title and immediately began to be compared to Jimmy Brown and Jim Taylor, two of the great heavy-duty carriers of the past.

Jefferson became the first rookie since Bob Hayes in 1965 to gain more than 1,000 yards (while tying a 26-year-old record held by Billy Howton with 13 touchdown receptions). And his name was linked with Lance Alworth's.

That, of course, had to happen. Lance Alworth was a flanker for the Chargers in the 1960s who became one of the American Football League's first nationally recognized stars. He gained more than 10,000 yards in 11 seasons and is a member of the Hall of Fame.

"I remember Lance," says Jefferson. "He was always getting open, had good hands, great concentration, just a great receiver. I have a lot to learn before I can be like him. But to compare me to

Lance is hard since his career is over and mine is, hopefully, just beginning. I watch and learn from all receivers. I can just about tell you what all have, but it's impossible to pattern yourself after just one player. Everyone has a different strength—one has height, another quickness, this one has lateral movement, the other speed."

While Jefferson obviously shies from comparisons to Alworth, there's little doubt the Chargers' receiver respects Alworth's achievements. But Alworth is ranked only sixth on the all-time receivers' list with 542 receptions and Jefferson isn't satisfied with that as his target. Chasing Charley Taylor's all-time record of 649 catches is more like it.

"I pretty much know what I can do," Jefferson says with matter-of-fact confidence. "My goal is being the leading receiver in NFL history. It'll take some doing. And you've got to be lucky with injuries. Charley Taylor had thirteen good years. But you [also] can reach that plateau by people saying you were the best."

There are some people, notably in San Diego, who already are saying that about the fleet, fluid 6-foot 1-inch, 198-pounder with hands like suction cups and the same unique ability Alworth had to leap high in the air for receptions.

"He amazes me every day," says quarterback Dan Fouts. "I'll throw a ball poorly and say to myself, 'Shoot, you missed that one.' Then I'll look up and Jefferson's caught it. I've never seen anybody go to the ball the way he does.

"He's also tough. He's not afraid to go over the middle. He'll lay his body out in any position to catch a ball. He has a lot of pride. He's not good, he's great. He's a superstar."

"He's just a fierce competitor," says coach Don Coryell. "He wants to succeed so much. Football is fun for him. He really gets fired up. He can hardly wait to practice. He works hard. And, like any great receiver, he can improve."

Jefferson accepts that kind of verbal applause graciously but it does make him a bit self-conscious. That's why he still isn't overjoyed when nicknames such as "the Jefferson Airplane" or "Lord Jeff" are applied. He'd prefer to simply be called J. J.

J. J. might have wound up at the University of Texas just as Campbell did, but he knew that coach Darrell Royal was committed to a philosophy based on the run. So he decided to join controversial Frank Kush at Arizona State instead.

"Arizona State threw the ball more than anyone I'd seen," Jefferson points out, "plus coach Kush had a reputation for sending receivers to the pros. I wanted to play where my abilities would be utilized. They also said he was tough, and I had to find out for myself. It turned out that he's not as tough as they said. I love the man."

The man also loves John Jefferson. "He's as tough as any football player I've ever had," Kush says. "I'm not just talking about receivers, either. I'm talking about football players, period. John will do whatever he has to do to catch the ball."

Jefferson enjoys being a wide receiver because he believes there isn't a job in football that's more "fun" than catching the ball. "Being in the pits [the line] isn't too much fun," Jefferson points out. "You get in all kinds of scraps. The backs have to take so many hits. The quarterback has so much to worry about. He's always under pressure.

"I like to work for catches. I like the ballet part of the game, and the fans like it, too." Particularly when the pirouettes are performed by a Lance Alworth or a John Jefferson.

Steve Largent

Wide Receiver, Seattle Seahawks

The Houston Oilers had made their top choices in the 1976 draft, and now it was time to make their fourth selection. Houston coach Bum Phillips decided to go for Tulsa receiver Steve Largent, the guy with the too-slow-to-make-it-in-the-NFL rap. Largent led the country in touchdown passes his junior and senior years with 14 each season, while surpassing most of the receiving records Howard Twilley had established at the pass-conscious university. The link with Twilley apparently cost Largent.

"I was always tagged with poor speed," Largent acknowledges. "I was compared with Howard Twilley and because Twilley didn't have good speed, they had to say I didn't either."

Phillips decided a fourth-round draft choice wasn't too big a risk to take a look at Largent. But he didn't look long enough at training camp, because Largent was quickly shipped to the Seattle Seahawks. The Oilers didn't even get their fourth-round draft choice back. They let Largent go for an eight-round selection. It was unquestionably one of the biggest steals in NFL history, and even Phillips acknowledges it.

"I wish I could talk about something more pleasant," Phillips says when he's asked about Largent. "That's my biggest goof ever on a player.

Opposite: *Earl Campbell rolls down the sideline. His remarkable
agility and great leg strength are captured in this freeze shot.*
Above: *Jerry Robinson (56) meets a Redskin opponent head to head.
Robinson's skill and determination give him Hall of Fame potential.*

That kid is a great football player. It looks like he's got a dip net when he catches the ball."

Largent's dip net brought him unmatched success before the NFL headed into the 1980s. In 1978, he caught 71 passes, more than any other wide receiver in the league. In 1979, he gained 1,237 yards, more than any other receiver in the league, fast or slow.

And, while John Jefferson, the San Diego receiver with the ability to leap high for the ball, is being compared to Lance Alworth, Largent is being compared to Fred Biletnikoff of the Oakland Raiders because of the precise routes he runs. Biletnikoff ran up and down NFL fields for 14 seasons catching passes and is ranked fourth on the all-time receivers' list with 589 receptions for 8,974 yards and a 15.2 average. Largent fully appreciates the comparison.

"I haven't modeled myself after Fred, but physically we have some of the same attributes," says Largent, a 5-foot 11-inch, 184-pounder, while Biletnikoff was 6-foot-1 and weighed 185 pounds. "And we both run disciplined routes and come back to the ball.

"I've always admired Fred as a player, his ability to catch the ball anywhere on the field. The most important aspect of a wide receiver is to catch the ball consistently, and Fred always made the big catch."

So does Largent, and coach Jack Patera knows that there is nothing to stop him from climbing up the ladder to challenge the best receivers in NFL history. "Years from now, you should be able to say he's had a great career," Patera says. "He should play in this league a long time. He hangs onto every thing thrown to him, whether it's in practice or a game. He doesn't have blinding speed, but he has enough to get behind the deep men, and I don't know if you need any more than that."

Jerry Rhome, who was Largent's college coach at Tulsa and coaches the quarterbacks and receivers at Seattle, is even more ecstatic.

"There are a lot of outstanding receivers in the NFL," says Rhome, "but I wouldn't trade Steve for any of them. He has a rare combination of ability, competitiveness, intelligence, durability, and he's a good influence on our team."

Rhome also tries to dispel the too-slow rap, which seems to rankle Largent. "Even now some people still ask me about Steve's speed," Rhome says. "I tell them to go ask the defensive backs who try to cover him. They know. I don't care what his time is in the forty. For sure, he's fast enough."

Largent doesn't depend on sheer speed or physical ability. He is a receiver who has tried to master his trade. "What I lack in physical ability I try to make up in technical ability," he explains. "And I try to keep myself alert. Part of being alert on the field is running consistent routes at proper depths and being where you're supposed to be at the right time. Instead of calling it a precision route-runner, I call it a disciplined route-runner. I just strive to be consistent and disciplined.

"A great tendency for players who have a lot of physical ability is to rely on that ability more than some of the technical things of route-running or catching the ball. You'll have a guy that's really fast and he might try to just run by somebody instead of running a good route or putting a move on and taking off.

"Ultimately I think it's more important to be a smart football player than it is to be fast or big or strong."

Ozzie Newsome

Tight End, Cleveland Browns

Ozzie Newsome always knew what he wanted to be when he was a youngster growing up in Muscle Shoals, Alabama. "I always was a ball freak—football, baseball, basketball," Newsome says. "I never did anything but play ball. I always wanted to play professional something, anything."

But, while Newsome knew what he wanted to be, it was Bear Bryant, the legendary coach at the University of Alabama, who simplified the selection process—and in a relatively simple manner. "I had to give up baseball and basketball when I went to Alabama," Newsome explains. "When you play for 'The Bear,' it's football the year 'round."

The decision to surrender to the Bear turned out to be the best decision Newsome ever made. He went on to become Alabama's "Wizard of Oz," accumulating 102 receptions, 2,070 yards, 16 touchdowns, and one of the most effusive send-offs Bryant has ever given any athlete. "He's the best end in Alabama history," said Bryant, "and that includes [Hall of Famer] Don Hutson." Bryant also singled out Newsome as the best athlete to play for the Crimson Tide since the revered Joe Namath left in 1964.

All that back-slapping left Newsome with the problem of taking his act into Cleveland as a first-round draft choice in 1978. It meant not letting himself or the Bear down, even though he was going to be shifted from wide receiver to tight end.

Newsome didn't let anyone down—not himself, not the Bear, not Browns' coach Sam Rutigliano. He grabbed 38 passes for 589 yards and a 15.5 average, became the first rookie to ever be named the team's offensive player of the year, and opened a wide vista that let everyone get a peek at his awesome potential.

Rutigliano spelled out Newsome's future at the time, a future most experts believe will make him the best tight end in the NFL. "It's amazing the contribution Newsome has made in almost every game," Rutigliano said. "And he has so much in front of him. Right now, he's doing everything on sheer talent. He's going to be even better in a year or two, when he refines the ability he's got."

Then Rutigliano made a revelation of more than passing interest, giving another indication of the regard for Newsome's talents in NFL circles. "Bum Phillips [coach of the Houston Oilers] told me," Rutigliano said, "they would have drafted Newsome first if they had not been able to make the deal [that enabled them to draft] for Earl Campbell."

Newsome, meanwhile, leaves no doubt that he will make himself just as comfortable at tight end as he was at wide receiver. "It's really not all that new to me," Newsome says. "I played tight end off and on for a number of years. I can still stand quite a bit of work, but I did play there some in high school and in eight or nine games as a junior in college. Besides, as a preacher once told me, 'Whatever you do, be the best at it,' and I'm here to try and be the best tight end in the business. It will take a while, but I'll work at it. Playing pro football has been the dream of my life. There is nowhere to go in football after this."

Newsome has worked at it, starting with building his body so that 232 pounds—15 more than in college—now fill out his 6-foot 2-inch frame. And he has worked on his blocking technique, critical for a tight end. "I like blocking," he says. "Making a key block on a touchdown makes me feel as good as scoring a touchdown—almost. The only difficult thing is that when you're a tight end somebody is always bothering you, trying to keep you off the ball."

But the best thing that ever happened to Newsome as far as he is concerned is the preparation he received at Alabama, because Bryant was so demanding. Newsome even suggests it was tougher at Alabama than it is in the NFL.

"That's something that surprised me when I first got here," he says. "It's easier here because there's not as much pressure as there was at Alabama and what pressure there is here is easier to deal with under coach Rutigliano. What I mean is that, at Alabama, we were like tin soldiers from Thursday to Saturday, before every game. But here, we're relaxed and don't feel pressure until just before the kickoff, and then it's all over."

What about the difference between the players in college and in the NFL? "The players in college and here are the same—all tough," Newsome says. "I wouldn't say they're physically better in the NFL, it's just that they're more experienced than in college. They know how to do things better.

"Like, in college football, you beat somebody on a pass route and he quits, and you get the ball. But here, they don't quit, they stay with you. In that respect, it's harder, a lot harder, because the players are more experienced. But I'm enjoying every minute of it, and I appreciate the Bear for getting me ready for the pros."

Steve Courson

Guard, Pittsburgh Steelers

Steve Courson stands 6 feet 1 inch tall, weighs in at 268 pounds, measures 56 inches around the chest, and has a story being told about him that may or may not be accurate.

The story concerns his wardrobe. Courson drapes his muscles primarily in T-shirts and jeans, but he supposedly does own one sports coat—which the Pittsburgh Pirates borrow to cover the infield during rain delays.

Whether the story is true or not, one thing is certain—the measurements for Courson are accurate. Not only the measurements but reports of the amazing feats he can accomplish, which include running the 40-yard dash in under five seconds and slam-dunking a basketball.

"People don't believe that I can dunk a basketball," Courson says with a smile. "Heck, I've been dunking since I was in junior high school. I've got great spring in my legs. I can lay my elbow on the rim. I get in schoolyard games and blow guys' minds.

"That's the misconception people have about weights. They see a big, muscular guy and they assume he's immobile. They say, 'Aw, he can't play, he's muscle bound.' That might be true, if all the

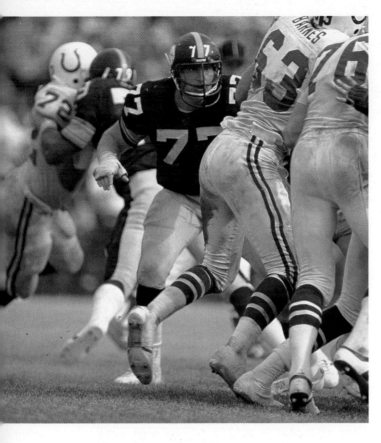

Above: *Steve Courson (77) at the guard position has quickness and strength to trap block or lead the end sweep. In school after four months on the weights he could press 400 pounds.* Opposite: *Jerry Robinson (56) fills the hole from his linebacker position and prepares to jump into the trenches against Washington.*

guy does is lift weights. But we lift weights, plus we stretch and run every day. We're as quick, as flexible as anybody on the team."

Courson certainly is, and that's why his nickname is unique among the Pittsburgh offensive linemen. As a unit, they're called "the Incredible Bulks," but Courson has been tagged "Sweeper," because when he pulls out from his guard position to lead a running back around end, he seems to suck up bodies like a vacuum cleaner gliding across a soiled rug.

This is the same guy that most scouts didn't think was worth a look when he was playing at South Carolina; they thought he was too short to make it in the NFL. The Steelers, however, happened to see him flatten someone during a Blue-Gray workout and decided he was worth a fifth-round draft choice.

He's worth quite a bit more now. Originally projected as a special teams player and a substitute, Courson continually refined his skills until his third season, in 1980, when he broke into the starting lineup. Now, he's headed for all-pro status.

And, according to Courson, it's weight lifting that has brought him to the threshold. "I always wanted to be a professional athlete," he points out, "but I never grew that much. I got around six feet and stopped. With me, the weights were a way of compensating. I remember reading the football magazines when I was a kid, looking at all the heights and weights. Everybody was six-three, two-thirty; six-five, two-fifty. I figured I had to take over where nature left off.

"I wound up going to high school in Gettysburg [Pennsylvania] and the coach there was Leo Ward. He was way ahead of his time when it came to weight training. When you signed up for the team, he tested you on this Universal gym. Got an idea how strong you were, how much you might develop. He said I had good natural strength. He said I could increase my weight a hundred pounds on each lift if I stuck with it. That was all I needed to hear. I started working out four hours a day. I would do every lift in the book and when I finished, I would invent a few of my own."

As the biceps bulged more and more, Courson was able to accomplish more and more. "Within three months I was pressing four hundred pounds," he says, "and I really came on as a football player. I got a few scholarship offers and took Carolina."

When he joined the Steelers, he admittedly was in awe. This was, after all, the team that had won more Super Bowls than any other in NFL history

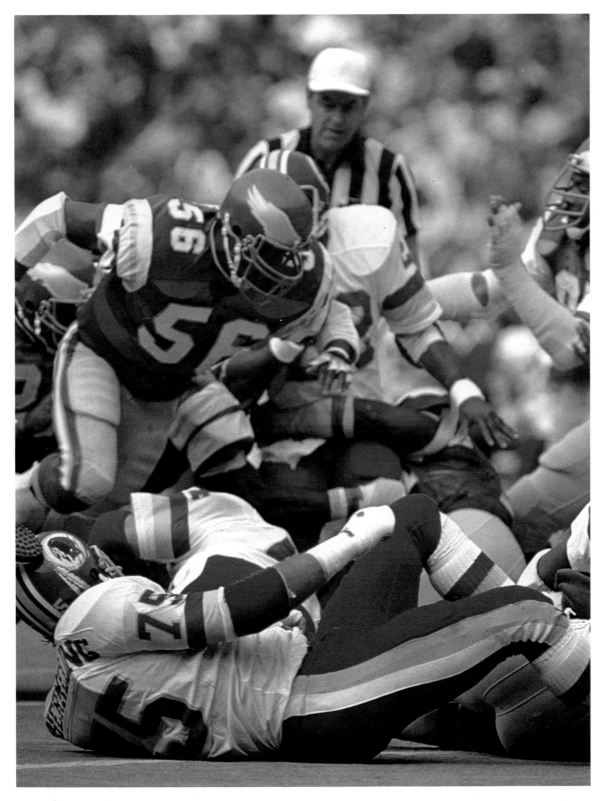

and whose list of players read like a Who's Who of professional football.

"I mean, being on the same team as Joe Greene was an honor," Courson says. "I think Joe is the greatest defensive player who ever played. I remember going up against him in training camp my rookie year. I never took so many bruises in my life. I'd be up against Joe one play, Ernie Holmes the next, Steve Furness the next. Those guys knocked me around like I was a pinball. It was a shock because I was used to crushing guys in college. I learned the pros are another world."

Now, of course, he's a member in good standing, particularly among the "Bulks." And he likes to express his feelings on behalf of all offensive linemen. "We're like a team within a team. I think that's true of most offensive lines. You don't get that much publicity. It's an area where most people don't really understand what goes on. You're up there beating your brains out on every play and you get the feeling the only guys who really appreciate what you're doing are the guys [on the line] around you. It makes us feel close, like brothers almost, because we know we're all in this together. I don't much care if the press makes a fuss over me as long as I know the other linemen know I did my job."

Dan Hampton

Defensive End, Chicago Bears

Doug Buffone, the former linebacker for the Chicago Bears, remembers the day he first learned what kind of defensive lineman teammate Dan Hampton was going to be.

"During a dummy scrimmage practicing a goal line stand, I was playing the part of the tight end," Buffone explains. "Hampton threw me down and tramped on me. He thought it was kind of funny. Big joke. He almost killed me."

Certainly the longtime veteran had words with the rookie from Arkansas, right? "What do you say to a two-hundred-sixty-pound animal, 'Pardon me, sir?'" Buffone questions. "I just got up and went back to the huddle. He had a funny smile on his face that reminded me of Dick Butkus."

The comparison may be more than incidental. Dick Butkus was the fierce, hard-hitting Chicago middle linebacker who terrorized offensive players during the late 1960s and early 1970s. Dan Hampton isn't a linebacker, but he figures to be as much of a terror during the 1980s.

It might help to understand what makes this 6-foot 5-inch stick of dynamite tick by knowing that his nickname is "Danimal"—a combination of his first name and animal. It also might help to know Hampton's description of himself. "I really wish I was about four different people. One to be in the band [he plays the saxophone and guitar]. One to play ball. One to sail. One to take a knife and a gun and go to Canada and see if I could live like an Indian.

"Indians always intrigued me the way they lived. Back in those days you more or less did what you wanted to. I think I would have been a better Indian than a citizen of the United States."

If that makes you believe that Dan Hampton finds it difficult to live and play in a conventional manner accepted by most people, then your assessment of Dan Hampton is 100 percent accurate. Dan Hampton is anything but conventional. He once wrestled an alligator in Florida. While he was growing up in Cabot, Arkansas, he was forever shooting "bottle rockets" at passing motorists while doing wheelies on his motorcycle. Everyone knew him, he says, as "that crazy Hampton boy on his motorcycle."

"All those pranks and stuff I've always done," he explains during a serious moment, "are just to lighten things up. The world is too serious nowadays. I never will cut out horsing around completely."

But he did make a concession so that he could play football—and play it well. "When football became an important thing," he says, "I cut down on some of the wild motorcycling. I figured you can't play a goal line defense from the emergency room."

Football didn't become an important thing until his junior year in high school. "I owe it all to my high school coach Bill Reed," Hampton says. "He found me in the school band. I had learned how to play the bass guitar and the alto sax and four other instruments. I used to play my guitar in the stands and switch over to the sax when we marched. Imagine me, a chubby little fellow of six-five and two-thirty, playing saxophone in the band. Reed kept looking at me like I was a piece of meat. When I was a junior, he pulled me out of the band and put me on the football team. Later, he made sure I went to Arkansas."

At Arkansas, Hampton made sure everyone became aware of him. He not only became an all-American, but played so well that the Bears took him as the fourth player selected in the draft. He returned immediate dividends by becoming an all-

"I love playing football," says Earl Campbell. "I even enjoy practicing. It's a job, I guess, a way of making a living, like nine to five. But the hours are better. . . ."

rookie selection, and there isn't anyone who thinks it will end there.

"He's the best rookie I've ever seen come through the Bear camp as a defensive lineman," says defensive tackle Jim Osborne, who has been around for a decade. "I've never seen a guy come to work as hard as Dan."

"He's so physically awesome," says safety Gary Fencik, "he just muscles his way past people." Alan Page, the only defensive player in NFL history to be voted MVP, concurs. "He picks up people and throws them around," Page says.

But it didn't start out that way for Hampton. Despite all the hoopla accompanying his arrival at the Bears' training camp, he was far from able to do his best when he was first thrown into NFL action.

"I was scared in those early games," he admits. "I was too concerned with not making mistakes. I was sitting back at the line and not coming to the ball. I was waiting for the ball to come to me. Now I've learned how to read plays, how to get off the line of scrimmage and go for the ball carrier."

But playing the run isn't what turns Dan Hampton on. What really makes it fun, he says, is when he knows he has a shot at the quarterback— and the quarterback doesn't know it.

"My biggest thrill in a game is blindsiding the quarterback," he says with a chuckle. "I just knock him backward. You catch him so quick you just knock him out."

Dick Butkus would love those sentiments.

Jerry Robinson

Linebacker, Philadelphia Eagles

Jerry Robinson knew he was going to be an athlete. He knew from the day his daddy, Floyd, an old cowboy from Henderson, Texas, began trying to convince his son that he should follow in his father's footsteps.

"He rode those Brahma bulls and did some calf-roping and bull-dogging," Robinson says, reminiscing about his father. "He's a construction worker now. He got older and realized he wouldn't be around much longer if he kept jumping off horses into cows with them big long horns. I remember he brought me a cowboy book home once. It had a picture on the cover of a cowboy on a horse, the horse rearing back. He talked to me about it, but I said to myself, 'No way, buddy, I'm

Opposite: *Phil Simms calls the signals for the New York Giants. On being a quarterback: "I know, if I reach my potential, I'll be one of the best in the NFL. I know that, so I feel an obligation to go for it." Above: John Jefferson, who may become the best receiver in NFL history. Dan Fouts says, "He'll lay his body out in any position to catch a ball. He has a lot of pride. He's not good, he's great."*

playing basketball and track and football.' "

Jerry Robinson may have recognized at an early age that it was harder to bring down a bronco at the rodeo than a Bronco in the open field, but it took him some time to make football his first priority. "When I was a kid, I didn't even like football," Robinson admits. "I just played it for something to do. You know, football was the first thing that came along in the fall, so I played it because I couldn't wait for basketball season to start. But it never interested me. I don't know why. I just didn't have a feeling for it."

What ultimately gave him the feeling was the fact that he couldn't see himself playing basketball when he had stopped growing at 6 feet 3 inches. "If I had to do it over again," he quips, "I'd grow an inch or two taller and be a basketball player."

Fortunately for the Eagles, it's too late for Jerry Robinson to grow taller. But there's no question he will be a bigger factor in the Philadelphia defense as he matures during the 1980s. Bill Bergey, the Eagles' longtime all-pro linebacker, insists Robinson will be among the best ever to play the position. "I'm excited just playing next to Jerry Robinson," Bergey says. "I mean it when I say he's going to go down as one of the all-time greats."

Coach Dick Vermeil, who recruited Robinson for UCLA, then drafted him for the Eagles, sounds just as enthusiastic as Bergey. "We drafted him because he was the best player in the country at his position, because he is a character individual, because he is a potential all-pro," Vermeil says. "I'll stake you anything you wanna stake he'll be a great player."

And, to complete the picture, add the words of assistant coach Lynn Stiles, who helped recruit Robinson for UCLA, and safety John Sciarra, who was the quarterback for the Bruins during Robinson's freshman year in 1976. "I saw him play high school nose guard and he was unstoppable," Stiles recalls. "He came to UCLA as a wide receiver and, by the time he was a sophomore, he was an all-American linebacker. The guy is just a tremendous athlete. He can do anything he wants to do out there."

"Our track coach, Jim Bush, wanted to make Jerry into a decathlon man," Sciarra remembers. "He said he never saw a guy with such a great combination of strength, speed, and agility."

Neither have the Eagles. That's why they've nicknamed Robinson "the Green Hornet." Green for the color of the Eagles' uniform. Hornet for the way he stings—quick and hard, from anywhere on the field. For if there's any one thing that sets Robinson apart from other linebackers, it's his unique ability to get from one point to another in record time. Outside linebackers are not expected to possess 9.7 speed for the 100. But Robinson does.

It's not naked speed, however, that is all Robinson has going for him. There's an extra ingredient—a commodity that Vermeil figured would make him a big-play defender able to achieve from his linebacking spot what Lynn Swann and Earl Campbell can from their offensive positions.

There are different labels for that commodity. Vermeil calls it "flash." Stiles calls it "explosion." Sciarra calls it "field awareness." Whatever it is, Jerry Robinson has it. He also has a great desire to succeed because of what happened in 1974 to his brother Jackie. Jerry Robinson, just 18 then, had no sooner walked into his house after a day in school when he was told Jackie had been shot in the head.

"He was with a couple of friends," Jerry Robinson explains. "They were messing with this gun and it accidentally went off." Jackie Robinson lingered in a coma for 14 months, then died.

Jerry Robinson had entered UCLA by then, but never said anything about his brother's death until the university's awards banquet during his senior year. At the banquet, Robinson was honored as a three-time all-American and his uniform number was retired. He obviously felt that was the time to do what he had to do, and when he walked to the microphone to accept his honors, he let it all out.

"This is for my brother Jackie," he said. "Everything I have done since his death has been for him."

There is no greater motivating factor for any athlete, any person.

Mike Haynes

Cornerback, New England Patriots

Mike Haynes had committed himself to Arizona State. But, after just one year, he was having second thoughts. He just didn't want to be a defensive back.

"I always wanted to be a receiver," Haynes explains. "As a kid in Los Angeles I idolized receivers. I was ready to transfer to Southern Cal or San Diego State after my freshman year. The coaches called me that summer and said I would play receiver. So I went back."

But it didn't work out the way Haynes expected. "We put Mike at cornerback as a freshman because we needed help there," remembers coach Frank Kush. "It was my intent to move him to receiver. But he was so valuable to us at cornerback he stayed there the full four years."

"The team needed me more on defense," Haynes says, recalling what happened when he returned for his sophomore season. "So I said the heck with it and worked as hard as I could at becoming a good defensive back."

The guy who didn't want to be a defensive back became so proficient at handling the demanding position that when the New England Patriots went looking for a cornerback in 1976, they tapped Haynes as the first defensive back they had chosen in the first round in a decade. They obviously knew what they were doing. No less an authority than Don Shula, the coach of the Miami Dolphins, said, "I have never seen a better cornerback than Mike Haynes."

The way Bucko Kilroy, the Patriots' director of player personnel, sees it, Mike Haynes is the rarest commodity in the world—a natural cornerback. "Cornerbacks," Kilroy points out, "must be quick, agile, fast, tough, and strong. They have to be able to run, jump, and tackle, all at the same time. You can't teach what they have to do. They're the shortstops of football."

It didn't take Haynes long to make his mark with the Patriots. The 6-foot 2-inch, 195-pounder immediately staked out a starting spot, intercepted eight passes, and was named Rookie of the Year in the American Conference.

Maybe it helped to have stayed at Arizona State, where he was subjected to the harsh regimen of the controversial Kush. It may have been even tougher for Haynes to get through Arizona State than his rookie season with the Patriots. "When we went to camp at Arizona State, we practiced three times a day," Haynes recalls. "During the season, we practiced twice a day, once in the afternoon, once at night.

"Then there was Kush's Mountain. It was this super-steep hill loaded with trees and thick weeds. If you made a mistake, like missing a tackle or jumping offside, he'd make you run the mountain after practice. The bad part was you had to run it after practicing for three hours and running for forty minutes. They say one player went up the hill and never came back. He just kept on running. The guy's probably running through the Arizona desert somewhere, forty years old, in a full football uniform, looking over his shoulder for Kush."

Would Haynes compare his experiences at Arizona State to those in the pros? "Pro football is a lot different from college," he says, "because it's more businesslike. It has a lot of politics and mental strain and going through ASU helped me prepare for all of that. Arizona State runs a pro system. Being a good player, being consistent and getting along with everybody is all part of it. I guess you could say that coping with all of that is political success. More than anything else in the pros, I've learned that anything can happen."

And it usually does at cornerback, which Haynes feels may be the toughest position to handle on a professional team. "Cornerback is a tough position to play—tougher than quarterback," Haynes insists. "I'm a little biased. I just know they don't pay cornerbacks like quarterbacks.

"If I get beat I just say to myself that that wasn't like me on that play. Then I go out there with the confidence that the next time I'll be ready. I like it when they pass a lot. I welcome those games."

Even when the opposition is passing a lot, Haynes may not get much action. The smarter quarterbacks have learned there's not much to gain by trying to pierce Haynes' area. Which leads one to believe Haynes may have some secret formula for success. Does he? "No," he replies. "You just go after the ball. The formation usually tips off whether the quarterback is going to throw or not, so once I see the ball in the air, I just go after it."

Sounds too simple, Mike. Isn't there anything else? Yes, admits Haynes, there is—watching belt buckles. "A receiver can move his shoulders and feet in a lot of different directions," Haynes explains. "But not the belt buckle. If I'm in proximity of the belt buckle, I'll be in good shape when the ball arrives."

5

Play Action

Preceding pages: *The Denver Broncos vs. the San Diego Chargers promises to be an exciting match-up in the eighties.* Above: *Neither rain nor sleet nor snow will keep these Oakland Raiders from their jobs or the fans from their enjoyment.* Opposite: *The old water bucket, wool jerseys, and leather helmets are things of the past. Today's equipment and uniforms are the products of space-age technology and rigorous safety standards. When worn by a 6'5", 250-pound player, the effect is impressive. Still, a man's gotta drink.*

Above: *The Pittsburgh Steelers are poised for the snap; the
Cincinnati Bengals' defense is set to spring; the effect is
an irresistible force meeting an immovable object. Opposite
(clockwise from top): Jim Zorn (10) hands off to Seattle
back Dan Doornink (33) as the 49er defense closes in; New
York Giants' defensive end Gary Jeter (70) meets St. Louis
Cardinals' tight end Garry Parris and neither player wants to
give an inch; if Ron Jaworski (7) hesitates, fleet-footed
Wilbert Montgomery (31) misses the handoff, but the play runs
because of constant practice and split-second timing.*

Below: *Stanley Morgan, wide receiver for the New England Patriots, stares the ball into his hands at the goal line with inches to spare.* Opposite: *Cedrick Hardman (86), defensive end for the San Francisco 49ers, gives as good as he gets in a game against the Green Bay Packers.* Following pages: *Any single match-up is a game within a game, and here's one of the best games in town—Philadelphia Eagle wide receiver Harold Carmichael (17) going against Oakland Raider cornerback Lester Hayes (37).*

Right: *Steve Bartkowski, QB for the Atlanta Falcons, shows the coolness a pro quarterback must have as he spins and looks for the handoff.* Opposite: *The kicking game is frequently the difference between a win and a loss. Oakland Raider Ray Guy is a master at punting the ball so that it hits a coffin corner.*

102

Opposite *(clockwise from top): The Louisiana Superdome sports a yellow ribbon for Super Bowl XV and the U.S. hostages' return to America; the Oakland Raiderettes; a fistful of XV tickets.* Above: *1981's Super Bowl XV, the game and the spectacle.*

6

Franchise Building

When Eddie LeBaron joined the Atlanta Falcons as their general manager in 1977, the club listed him in its press guide as being 5 feet 9 inches tall. It didn't take long for everyone to realize that while you generally put on weight as you put on years you normally don't gain height—and Eddie LeBaron had been a 5-foot 7-inch quarterback for 11 NFL seasons.

How did he grow two inches? "The height [in the press guide] is wrong," LeBaron explained. "They must have gone back to some old Redskin roster for that. George Preston Marshall [the Washington Redskins owner] said that a five-foot seven-inch quarterback couldn't play in the NFL,

so he insisted that I be listed as five-nine."

No matter what LeBaron was listed at, he did play at 5 feet 7 inches, a fact that alarmed his wife when she first realized the actual size of the mammoth maulers who were trying to bend and batter his body. That occurred when she met him outside the dressing room after he had quarterbacked the West team to a narrow victory over the East in the 1956 Pro Bowl. As LeBaron stood there making small talk, Big Daddy Lipscomb of the East team sidled up to the little quarterback and stared down menacingly.

"My wife hadn't been around football much," LeBaron recalls. "Big Daddy was six-nine and

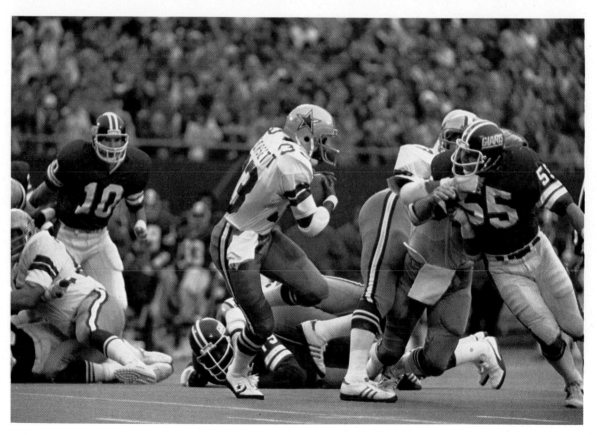

Preceding pages: *Bradshaw (12) hands to Harris (32) as Pugh (75) blasts through. Pittsburgh and Dallas built dynasties on the college draft.* Above: *Dallas' #33, Touchdown Tony Dorsett.* Right: *Charlie Johnson (65), running back for the Philadelphia Eagles.*

weighed three hundred pounds. He had a little beard and he wore a pork pie hat. Sweat was pouring down his goatee. He loomed over me and said, 'You little son of a gun, I'll get you next year.' Hell, my wife wanted me to quit right on the spot."

LeBaron, however, was anything but a quitter either as a player or as a lawyer in Las Vegas after he left football. And, while he may have been a little quarterback for the Redskins and Cowboys, he's become a big man for the Falcons—even without those extra two inches.

LeBaron's adoption of the franchise-building philosophies of the two dominant dynasties of the 1970s—the Dallas Cowboys and the Pittsburgh Steelers—have made the Falcons one of the teams to keep more than a casual eye on during the eighties. LeBaron took over at Atlanta in 1977 after the Falcons had won 11 games in three previous seasons, and just four short years later they were division champions for the first time in the team's 15-year history.

Eddie LeBaron at Atlanta, Dick Vermeil at Philadelphia, Chuck Knox at Buffalo—all three brought their teams home as division winners in 1980 for the first time since the premerger days of the 1960s. LeBaron is a general manager, Vermeil and Knox coaches, but they get the major share of the credit here because they are in total charge of the football operations of their clubs—they have established the philosophical priorities.

And all three did it with much the same approach, admittedly borrowed from the Cowboys and Steelers, by relying on the annual draft of college players to refurbish teams that had fallen into their respective division cellars.

Vermeil came out of the college coaching ranks, leaving UCLA for Philadelphia, where he took over the Eagles after they had languished in the NFC East cellar with a 4–10 record in 1975. Knox came to Buffalo from the Los Angeles Rams, joining the Bills following a 1977 season in which they hit bottom in AFC East at 3–11.

LeBaron took a far less conventional route. When Falcon owner Rankin Smith called, LeBaron had a successful law practice in Las Vegas that, coupled with profitable wine vineyards in California, provided LeBaron with a comfortable life-style. Nevertheless, LeBaron was intrigued with the idea of running an NFL franchise, even if it was one that had fallen into the NFC West basement with a 4–10 record in 1977.

"Primarily I wanted to get back to something I love—football," he explains. "I wouldn't give up a successful law practice on a whim. And, I didn't take the job as a stop-gap measure. It was something I really thought I could get into. The more I thought about it [after Smith approached him], the more I became fascinated. Football is still basically football, but it's like a lot of other endeavors. You have to find the best responsible people and let them have responsibility within the framework and policy that you have set for the organization. My philosophy [in law] was to find the best lawyers. In football my philosophy is to find the best football players."

There is no doubt where he stands when it comes to the subject of how to take a loser and make it a winner. "The teams that are good and stay good do it through the draft," LeBaron says. "I'm talking about teams like Pittsburgh, Dallas, and Los Angeles. You can't sacrifice tomorrow for today. George Allen made it go in Washington by giving up future draft choices for players. But I don't think that works often."

He won't get any argument from Vermeil or Knox. "Dick Vermeil is a student of the game," Eagles' general manager Jim Murray emphasizes, "and as a student of the game he did a study of the Cowboys and a study of the Steelers. They showed how many top draft choices the championship teams had. Vermeil said he was convinced the only way to build was the draft."

"You always want to emulate the successful people," Knox says. "The teams that have had the greatest success in the last decade of professional football—the Cowboys and Steelers—were built primarily through the college draft. This is often not the quickest route but it is the surest."

"It is my theory," says LeBaron, "you have to turn over a club every seven years. Now that doesn't mean everybody has to go. Some players reach their peaks in their seventh through twelfth years. But what I mean by turning over is that each year you must add seven to nine new people."

Gil Brandt, the vice-president in charge of personnel for the Cowboys, looks at the subject of turnover in a slightly different manner. According to Brandt, the ideal makeup of an NFL club includes a balance of players with six or more years of experience to "stabilize" the team, those with three to six years experience who are the "producers," and the remainder "enthusiastic" rookies and second-year men.

Until Knox arrived at Buffalo, it was no secret that the Bills were one of the worst if not *the* worst drafting teams in the league. Knox completely dis-

Ernie Holmes, one of the 12 players selected from the ranks of college players in 1971 who made the Steeler team. In 1974 Pittsburgh picked Swann, Lambert, Stallworth, and Webster.

mantled the Bills' scouting program and rebuilt it in his image. The result: 19 players from the draft made the Bills in his first three years. "I wanted to reorganize the scouting operations totally," Knox says. "I brought in Norm Pollom, who successfully ran four of the five drafts while I was in Los Angeles, and then set out to devise a system that would give us as complete coverage of talent as any team in the league.

"There are different layers of cross-checking that minimize your chance of error. First, we belong to BLESTO [scouting combine] and we pay around fifty-five thousand to sixty thousand dollars for their services. They have scouts who live in the center of a specific geographic area, and each covers every college in his area. Each scout's report is forwarded to teams in the combine. If a school doesn't have any pro prospects, we'll get a report saying that. In effect, all colleges in the country are covered and a lot of legwork is eliminated.

"The BLESTO reports are the beginning. Then our scouts go out and look at players in spring practice, during practice and games in the fall, and see film.

"The next layer of cross-checking is the sifting-out process, where we look at the top one hundred players. One scout will cover east of the Mississippi River and another will cover the West. They will evaluate the players and send back reports.

"The layer after that is to have another scout see all one hundred himself. Suppose there are two players rated highly by BLESTO and our [regional] scouts. Come draft day, who do we take? That's why it's important to have a third scout see all one hundred. He would have the final say [on draft day] since he has seen both players."

The two most impressive examples of what the draft can do for a team involve the Steelers. In 1971, the Steelers selected so well that 12 players they drafted made the team and two made other NFL teams. Included among the players sticking with the Steelers were linebacker Jack Ham, defensive end Dwight White, defensive tackle Ernie Holmes, safety Mike Wagner, and tackle Larry Brown.

The Steelers may have topped that in 1974. Their number-one draft pick was wide receiver Lynn Swann. Middle linebacker Jack Lambert was selected on the second round. The Steelers didn't have a third-round pick, but when the fourth came around they went for wide receiver John Stallworth. The Steelers had one more fourth-round se-

lection and used it to grab defensive back Jimmy Allen (now a starter with the Detroit Lions) before finishing things off with a fifth-round pick that enabled them to snare center Mike Webster.

The Pittsburgh philosophy, says coach Chuck Noll, is basically simple. "Everyone says I'm unpredictable in my drafting," Noll says. "But I'm very predictable, if people would just listen. We're not necessarily looking for players to fill specific needs. We're looking for the best players. Our theory is to draft the best available athlete. That will explain why we took Swann when we already had Ron Shanklin, Frank Lewis, and others on the squad at the wide receiver positions. When we drafted, he was the best all-around player available. It makes no sense to settle for anything else. It would be narrow-minded of us to sit down and decide we need a linebacker, then find our top two or three candidates already chosen and pick beneath them. If we can't use a defensive end, for instance, we're sure someone else can [and the Steelers can trade him for a draft choice]. But if he's that good, we'll use him."

There can't, however, be any deviation from the plan according to the Steeler method of operating. "There has to be a commitment to building through the draft," says Steeler vice-president Art Rooney, Jr. "You can't just say you're going to build through the draft and go trading a year later."

The base for the Steelers is the BLESTO scouting combine. The Steelers were a charter member, along with Chicago, Detroit, Philadelphia, and Minnesota. The total grew to include Miami, Baltimore, Buffalo, and Kansas City. "They [BLESTO] give you the information, but you still have to interpret it," Rooney points out. "You have to take it position by position. You look at the critical factors on each player, in the spring and fall, for twenty-two positions. Each position takes at least an hour. It's very boring work—but it's also been very rewarding work."

Noll, however, is not as predictable as he says he is because, while he never deviates from his best-athlete principle, he does deviate from other standards that have been established as yardsticks by combines or teams.

"A lot of scouting combines come in and say guards should have such and such dimensions and linebackers such and such dimensions," Noll says. "We'd probably be substandard in most of the areas. I mean, they say tackles are supposed to be six-foot-four and we've had a lot of tackles about

Preceding pages: Atlanta vs. L.A. In the eighties, linebackers will be quicker, offensive linemen will be bigger. Left: The Eagles' outstanding defensive end, Carl Hairston (78).

113

six-two. We don't have dimensions like that. We look for somebody who stands out, somebody who has something special. Mike Wagner had exceptional strength. Jack Lambert had exceptional tenacity. Lynn Swann had exceptional leaping ability."

Pittsburgh's principles may continue to remain the same, but the general feeling among NFL personnel experts is that the opportunity to pull off draft coups like the Steelers did in 1971 and 1974 will not be available to teams drafting in the eighties. The major reason is the success of the Steelers and Cowboys due to the draft. With so many teams becoming carbon copies and relying so heavily on the draft, the same opportunities that existed in the seventies just don't exist any more.

"Everybody is doing such a good job [drafting], it's tough for any one team to have a draft that dramatically improves the team," says Gil Brandt. "There are almost no bad mistakes being made. Look at the first two rounds of 1980—only one guy [who was drafted] isn't active. What has probably happened is that the draft has become overvalued. People have looked at the teams that have been successful—Pittsburgh, Dallas, Los Angeles, Philadelphia, Atlanta, Buffalo—and seen that they have been predominantly building by drafting, so they now have a great reluctance to give up a draft choice.

"We have created a monster with so much talk about teams being draft-built. The draft that started in 1936 with Jay Berwanger being the first player ever selected is doing what it set out to do—create parity. It wasn't really until the late 1970s that the philosophy of building through the draft was adopted by *all* teams. Even in the early 1970s there was plenty of trading going on for established players when a coach thought he might be able to save his job by getting immediate help [and having his team improve, at least temporarily] rather than building."

The Cowboys, unlike the Steelers, have indulged in trading, particularly when a critical player is involved. The most publicized case in which Dallas surrendered choices for a player occurred in 1977 when the Cowboys, coveting Heisman trophy winner running back Tony Dorsett, shipped their number-one draft choice and three number twos to Seattle for the Seahawks' number-one pick. The Seahawks' selection—the second pick in the entire draft—elevated the Cowboys high enough for them to be able to grab Dorsett.

The Houston Oilers pulled off a similar coup

a year later and made University of Texas running back Earl Campbell the number-one choice in the entire draft.

Brandt doubts trades like that—involving the top draft choices that can make or break teams—will be as commonplace in the future. "The Dorsett and Campbell trades put both the teams involved in the playoffs," Brandt emphasizes. "Dallas actually went to the Super Bowl because of it. It's harder now to make a trade to get that type player who will give you the push needed to put a team in the playoffs.

"What has happened is that a number-one draft choice has become so big, so important, that you not only have to justify trading a number-one choice for a player to the owner of the club, but also to the city involved, or the adverse publicity could be terrible."

It's not quite the same when a number one isn't involved, but Brandt feels draft choices have become so valuable to clubs that they are reluctant to let them go even when legitimate talent is offered in return. "Look at Chuck Muncie," says Brandt, pointing to the running back New Orleans traded to San Diego during the 1980 season. "He was the fifth player picked overall in the draft [his senior season] and all New Orleans could get for him was a second-round choice and not a high one at that. It's extremely difficult to get market value for a player you want to trade [if draft choices are involved]. There might very well be an eventual swing back to the George Allen way [trading draft choices for veteran players] of doing it. You'd give up a number two for a top player, a third for a good player, a fourth for a player just a notch below."

While Brandt—and the Cowboys—now believe the draft has become "overvalued," the Oakland Raiders have been operating with that in mind as long as Al Davis has been the architect of their player-acquisition philosophy.

The Raiders, who after winning Super Bowl XI underwent repairs and resurfaced before most expected them to and won Super Bowl XV, are the only one of the NFL's 28 clubs that does not belong to any scouting combine. They go it alone, and they do it their own way. "We just believe there are certain plusses in doing things our own way," explains Al LoCasale, the Raiders' executive assistant and Davis' right-hand man. "We operate [in securing personnel] on an Al Davis maxim, 'I'd rather be right than consistent.' Al never says always and never says never."

That philosophy has made the Raiders the

most difficult team in the NFL to categorize. It should also be pointed out that they are one of the most successful; the Raiders haven't had a losing season since 1964.

"There are four sources of players," says Lo-Casale. "There's the draft, trades, college free agents, and pro free agents. Our 1980 team had ten players on it who had been acquired by trade—seven in 1980 alone. You can't get fixed into a position that has no flexibility. You can't take the George Allen approach that one way to build is the only way. Most teams rely on the draft because you're guaranteed twelve picks. But there are *other* sources."

One of the other sources is players who, for one reason or another, have been cast off by other teams, often because they are hard to handle or difficult to discipline. The Raiders seem to delight in such reclamation projects. "We are very willing here to take people other people don't want," Lo-Casale acknowledges. "We are looking for people to help us win. We are not looking for reasons not to take people. We do take some people other teams wouldn't take. We also take some people at a different level than some others would consider."

The best example of this is punter Ray Guy. When Guy was drafted by the Raiders, he became the first punter ever drafted on the first round. "We rely on using people's strengths," LoCasale explains. "We rely on doing what we think is right.

"We gave up two first-round draft choices for [linebacker] Ted Hendricks and we wouldn't have been in Super Bowl XI without him. We'll take an older guy like [defensive lineman] Cedrick Hardman and use him in situations in which he does best what we ask him to do. We also have a willingness to make changes—we switched Billy Cannon from a running back to tight end and Hewritt Dixon from a tight end to running back.

"Al has said the draft is overrated," LoCasale continues. "He doesn't mean it isn't a prime source of material, he means what's more important is what you do with them [players] after you draft them [developing players, converting them to other positions]. It's not hard to succeed with the Dorsetts, it's the other people that you have to concern yourself with.

"We want to get people here and develop them in our traditions and our style. And you can see the difference when it happens. Some have had a tradition of losing . . . they may not realize it, but they have. They finally begin to realize that it's not that way here, that there's a winning tradition here."

That was missing at Philadelphia until Vermeil took over after the club had suffered nine consecutive seasons in which they were unable to climb over .500. Vermeil took the Eagles from the NFC East cellar to the Super Bowl with what may very well be the fewest top draft choices in history. "No team that I know as depleted of high draft choices as ours was has ever been so successful," says Jim Murray. "Dick is like Lombardi—a fundamentalist. Our success is directly attributable to him and his ability to teach and bring in assistants who can teach."

The Eagles made it to the Super Bowl in 1980, the fifth year of Vermeil's reign. During that time, of course, the team participated in five drafts, but only two number ones were left from the preceding regime. Vermeil used them to add two players—linebacker Jerry Robinson and cornerback Roynell Young—who have become starters. But he also has taken a number of middle-round draft choices and turned them into stars.

Running back Wilbert Montgomery was a sixth-round draft choice and standout defensive linemen Charley Johnson and Carl Hairston were seventh-rounders. Wide receiver Harold Carmichael (on the roster when Vermeil arrived) was also a seventh-rounder. "Dick's philosophy is to take average people and coach the hell out of them," says Sid Gillman, formerly one of his chief assistants. "With the way the draft is now, he's right. The talent is so spread out, so limited."

Gillman says there usually are no more than four or five superstars coming out of college every year, no more than a dozen truly outstanding players, and no more than two dozen good players available. "That's only about forty players in all," he estimates. "That doesn't even get you halfway through the second round of the draft now. So what you've got to do is coach the hell out of everybody else."

Having experienced failure under Mike McCormack, who tried to build the George Allen way, the Eagles now guard their draft selections like rare jewels. But even the Eagles are not reluctant to deviate from the norm if the proper situation presents itself. "It would take something exceptional for us to trade away our top choices," says Murray. "But you've got to be flexible enough if the opportunity arises to take advantage of it."

Murray cites the acquisition of pass-rushing defensive end Claude Humphrey as an example. When he became available, the Eagles were more than willing to send Atlanta draft choices in exchange. They were a pair of number fours, however. Number ones remain locked in the vault.

If there is a formula for building a winner, it would seem that it's to hold onto your top draft choices, make sure you use them wisely when selecting talent, and keep your mind open if a trade opportunity comes your way. Any team must, however, be cognizant of the fact that players put up for trade are often players who have had difficulties with the clubs offering them around. The Raiders don't seem to shy from dealing in those situations; others do.

Once all those players are in hand, the next step is to make them better than when you acquired them—and that is what Vermeil has done so well and what Brandt says all teams will have to do better in the future. And it's likely that those teams which learn how to accomplish that the best—those who have the best teachers—will be the most successful in the 1980s.

"It's like anything else, like department stores," says Brandt. "All along there are only so many of them and then, suddenly, there's a K-Mart and there's a lot more competition, so all the others have to find better ways to merchandise. That's what we're going to be doing in the 1980s. We have to find better ways to evaluate talent, better ways to develop talent, better ways to make talent stronger. Anything to get the edge over somebody else.

"Sid Gillman [when he was the coach of the San Diego Chargers] was the first guy to hire a strength coach. Now there's one on almost every team. Then we went to flexibility guys. We're always moving into new areas. Now it's scouting—we're getting a much better type of person associated with scouting. Now the people involved in scouting aren't coaches who have been fired from their jobs who are going to scout for a couple of years to get their pension before retiring. Now we're hiring sharp, aggressive guys. We've become better in that way."

Recognizing that the game has changed from one that has been run-oriented to one that now relies heavily on the pass, says Brandt, will change—in a major way—the kind of players teams will be looking to add to their rosters. "This is a passing era," Brandt emphasizes. "There will be different offensive linemen and different linebackers and different defensive backs than in the Miami big-back era when they ran the ball almost every play and threw only ten to twelve times a game.

"We're no longer looking to find the two-hundred-pound defensive back to take down a [Larry] Csonka, we're looking for the one-hundred-eighty-five-pound guy who can run like heck and cover a [John] Jefferson. The linebackers will have to be quicker to cover running backs coming out of the backfield [for passes]. I don't know if a [Dick] Butkus or a [Ray] Nitschke would be as dominating factors today as they were when they played.

"Offensively, the most important thing today because of the passing game is pass protection. There will, therefore, have to be a trend to a bigger, stronger guy who can protect the passer. With quarterbacks throwing for three hundred and four hundred yards every game, passing is what you have to do to win. If you have the choice between a two-hundred-fifty-pounder and a two-hundred-ninety-pounder, you'll take the two-hundred-ninety-pounder. He may be slower, but he'll be bigger and stronger."

Brandt also foresees the day—although not in the immediate future—when sophisticated testing procedures will enable the new breed of sharp, aggressive scout to examine a draft choice's psyche, as well as his time for the 40-yard dash. "The popularity of the sport allows us to be a lot more innovative than if we weren't successful," Brandt says. "For example, with the problems Ford Motor Company is having, you wouldn't expect them to spend a lot of money innovating. Innovative things are costly. But we can afford to remain innovative. In-depth studies are being done now trying to find characteristics for success. Psychological testing isn't refined enough yet, but it wouldn't surprise me if we could put together a successful test that would point to guys who can't make it."

Admittedly, however, the Cowboys and other NFL teams are not even close to a breakthrough for such a testing procedure. There just haven't been any significant developments in that arena yet. Height, weight, time—yes. Heart, mind—no. And there isn't a coach in the business who wouldn't welcome some computerized assistance when it comes to being able to judge a player's character. They're all basically looking for the same things in every player acquired either by draft or trade.

"The country is full of good coaches," explains Don Coryell of the San Diego Chargers. "What it takes to win is a bunch of interested football players. The personnel is about even on most teams. Where they differ is in the way they concentrate. The winners are the real determined battlers, the guys who never give up, who have what it takes to come from behind, who will hang in there and

make something happen at the end of the game.

"The thing I preach is that I'm looking for football players who give all they've got. I want them to give everything they've got all the time, no matter who they play, no matter what the score. There are a lot of ball players around who do that but, unfortunately, not all of them are the best players. Very often in the past I've gone with lesser players. You win more games with that type of player in the long run. At least you're not so apt to lose games you should have won."

And, now, let's listen to Chuck Noll, who after all was the most successful coach of the seventies. "We look for guys who fit in with one another, and that takes time to find out," Noll says. "We're after people who fit in and complement one another. This is a team sport. You have to be able to function as a team and you have to learn to do that over a period of time.

"We are looking, of course, for athletes—that's number one. We're looking for people with speed, quickness, agility, strength. But we're also looking for people with the ability to learn. I think our football players also have to have a sense of responsibility. They know they have to be at their best because the guy next to him is busting his butt to do his best. And we're after people who want to be the best—not necessarily the best paid—but the best at their positions. Some guys just want to work hard enough to become the highest paid and then they rest on their laurels. But we want guys who just care about being and remaining the best.

"You change every year, subtly. You grow with the game. The game is a growing, living thing, and you grow with it."

Above: *Al Davis, owner of the Oakland Raiders, is a man who walks alone. Oakland is the only NFL team that does not belong to a scouting combine. Davis finds important roles for players cast off from other clubs.* Left: *Steelers' chairman of the board Art Rooney, Sr. Rooney is a firm believer in building with the draft. The Steeler success has made other teams reluctant to trade first-round choices for players.*

7

The Fun of It

Quarterback Ken Anderson sat down for a quiet moment with his four-year-old son Matt before bedtime one night just after his Cincinnati Bengals had completed a 4–12 season that definitely left something to be desired. But, if nothing else, the end of the season at least brought a respite from the fury of the football field, and time for those cherished moments with family. And, so, this evening, Ken Anderson asked his son if he knew what he wanted to be when he grew up. "Yes, daddy," Matt said. "I want to be a football player."

Anderson felt an immediate surge of pride, as do most parents whose children want to follow in their footsteps. Anderson proceeded to ask his son if he had a particular team in mind he wanted to play for when he was old enough.

"I don't know," Matt replied.

"What about the Bengals?" Anderson asked.

"Nope," Matt replied. "They always lose."

• • •

No one ever would have known what happened to the Oakland Raiders before Super Bowl XI—in which they whipped the Minnesota Vikings 32–14—if coach John Madden hadn't ultimately come clean. But Madden did, when he left coaching and became a TV analyst.

The Raiders had spent the week getting ready for the Super Bowl in Newport Beach, California, which Madden finally realized was so far from the Rose Bowl—site of the game—that it could take the Raiders a number of hours to get there on Super Sunday. So he had owner Al Davis arrange to get the Raiders rooms in Los Angeles the night before the game. But, even after they had registered, Madden's fears about the ride to the Rose Bowl still hadn't been fully alleviated. "We were a half hour from the Rose Bowl," Madden explained. "I could see the Raider bus stalled on the freeway while the Vikings won Super Bowl XI by forfeit."

At the team's breakfast meeting, Madden told the players they would leave for the Rose Bowl with plenty of time to spare, at 9:45 A.M. The ner-

vous coach got to the team bus well before that, took his seat, and waited, admittedly impatient. "Everyone, or so I thought, boarded the bus at nine-thirty," Madden said. "Just then, a guy in a pirate uniform with an eagle beak tried to climb aboard. I asked him where he was going. He said he was volunteering to be our mascot, sit on the bench, and help me run the team. I told him to get out of the bus, but he begged, pleaded, and almost drove me nuts. So I slammed the door on him and told the driver to move out. Two helicopters and a police escort ushered us toward the stadium.

"I checked the players . . . once, twice, three times. I couldn't believe it. Five were missing—a linebacker, a kick return specialist, two ball carriers, and six-foot-eight, two-hundred-ninety-pound John Matuszak, who represented one-third of our defensive line. You've got to understand things like that don't happen to professional football teams. I coached twenty years and not one player was ever left at the hotel before a game. Yet on Super Bowl Sunday, the biggest day of my life, I had left five players behind. When we reached the stadium, I was really sweating. I went out on the field, looked around corners, into showers and bathrooms. No players. I had to tell someone, so George Anderson, our trainer, lent me his ear."

"I goofed," Madden told Anderson. "I'm missing five players, including one-third of the defensive line."

"Don't worry, coach," Anderson replied. "They're here."

"Where in hell are they?" Madden bellowed.

"Hiding from you, coach," Anderson said. "They were in the lobby, trying to get rid of their extra tickets when the bus left."

"How'd they get here?" Madden boomed.

"One of them took a cab," Anderson said. "Another a cop's car. The last three came with the crazy guy in the pirate uniform."

"You know," Madden points out when he tells the story, "I never told anyone at the time—not a soul—that I had that bus leave fifteen minutes ear-

Preceding pages: *John Madden, former coach of the Oakland Raiders, is carried off the field victoriously by his players.* Right: *Ken Anderson's son wants to be a football player when he grows up.*

ly. The players thought they were lucky not to have been fined."

• • •

Jim Zorn was being questioned about the perils of being a scrambling quarterback in the NFL. "You have to know when and how to go down," Zorn pointed out. "The key is to have a fervent desire to be in on the next play."

• • •

The Detroit Lions were in Cincinnati to play the Bengals in an exhibition game and, when they arrived at their hotel, placekicker Benny Ricardo decided he wanted to head straight for his room and sack out. He thought it was strange when he went to the room and his roommate failed to show up, but he didn't think about it for long, slipped into the bed, and soon fell asleep.

He slept until about 3 A.M. when he heard laughter in the hall and a key turn in the lock to his room. Before his eyes had become accustomed to the darkness, the door flew open and something landed on top of him.

There was considerable scrambling at that point—before Benny realized what had happened and why his roommate hadn't shown up. Benny had been given the wrong room. The room he had been sent to had been assigned to a honeymoon couple—the groom had just opened the door, carried his bride across the threshold, and thrown her on the bed.

• • •

Bum Phillips, the coach of the Houston Oilers, stood up at his weekly press conference one morning and told about the woman who had approached him before a recent game.

"The lady came up to me and told me her husband had died," Phillips said. "She wanted me to give his Oiler ticket to someone. I asked her why she just didn't give it to one of his friends and she said, 'I would, but they're all at the funeral.'"

• • •

Every year, every Thanksgiving, NFL rookies in a number of cities fall prey to the old Turkey Trot. The game is simple: the veterans tack a notice up on the team's bulletin board announcing that all players are being provided turkeys for the holiday. They're free, offered by a fan of the team who just happens to be a turkey farmer. There's only one catch—the players have to pick up the turkeys themselves. And they have to pick them up at a turkey farm halfway across the state.

There are, however, always rookies anxious to obtain something for free and running back Mike Pruitt of the Cleveland Browns admits he was one of the turkeys chasing a free bird his rookie season. Pruitt drove all the way to the required turkey farm with several other first-year players, only to be confronted by an incredulous turkey farmer who reacted as if he were face to face with several guys slightly off center. "I don't know anything about free turkeys," he insisted over and over again.

"They [the veterans] set it up so well," said Pruitt. "They had a list and all the players signed their names. They even put down how much they wanted their turkey to weigh. We bit at the bait and they reeled us in. I got up at seven A.M. to make that [long] drive. I could have used the sleep."

• • •

Mike Barnes, a defensive tackle for the Baltimore Colts, had just been asked how old he was. The question certainly seemed simple, but Barnes hesitated before answering. Then he finally replied.

"Chronologically, I'm twenty-seven, but in the NFL you age in dog years. What is it, seven dog years to one human year? And I'm even older. It's double dog years for defensive linemen."

• • •

Tommy Bell was an NFL referee for 18 seasons, but despite his longevity he had no trouble singling out the strangest play he'd ever seen. It centered around Fred Arbanas, who played tight end for the Kansas City Chiefs with one glass eye.

Arbanas was hit extremely hard on the play Bell remembered, and Bell noticed something fall to the ground. It was Arbanas' glass eye. "I didn't know what was going on when I first saw it looking up at me from the AstroTurf," Bell recalled. "I picked it up and held it while the doctor revived Arbanas. When he was up, I handed him the eye.

"A water boy had a bucket handy, and Arbanas just swirled it around in the water and then slapped it right back in his head just like he would a contact lens. I said, 'Golly, Arbanas, you got a lot of guts. What would you do if your other eye was injured?' He didn't even crack a smile. He said, 'Mr. Bell, I'd become a referee just like you.'"

• • •

John Brodie used to double as the holder for

placekicks when he was quarterbacking the San Francisco 49ers, and one day a reporter decided to investigate the situation.

"Why," asked the reporter, "as one of the NFL's top quarterbacks, are you relegated to holding the football on conversion and field goal attempts?"

"Because," said Brodie, "if I didn't it would fall down."

• • •

His real name was Joe Don Looney, and there were those who say his surname fitted him perfectly. A running back from Oklahoma with considerable talent, he never was able to make it big in the NFL because of his considerable ability to torment the coaches he played for with his antics.

During one game while he was a member of the Detroit Lions, Harry Gilmer yelled for Looney to get off the bench as he called a play from the sidelines. Then Gilmer told Looney to take the play into the huddle. "If you want a messenger boy," Looney said, "call Western Union."

While he wasn't happy being a messenger, Looney didn't particularly see the need for all the practice the pros indulged in. So Detroit linebacker Joe Schmidt tried to explain how important he thought it was.

"I've never missed a practice in twelve years with the Lions," Schmidt said.

"Hey, Joe," Looney retorted, "you owe it to yourself to take a day off."

Looney eventually drifted to Atlanta, where, before he left to join the army, he tortured coach

Cleveland quarterback Brian Sipe gathers his teammates around him to orchestrate the next play—or perhaps the team is planning how to outfox the rookies at the next Turkey Trot.

Norm Van Borcklin. Heaving a sigh of relief, Van Brocklin made a prediction. "Give the army two weeks," he said, "and they'll have him on waivers."

• • •

Coach Bum Phillips of the Houston Oilers was musing about passing a physical examination.

"Now," he said, "if I drop dead tomorrow, at least I know I died in good health."

• • •

The Tampa Bay Buccaneers began play in the NFL in 1976 and put together an 0–14 record that had their fans totally exasperated. That didn't keep the team from doing its best to keep the fans turned on in the off season by sending public relations people to speak at a number of functions.

One official addressed a group of senior citizens and told them nothing but the facts—that expansion teams usually experienced growing pains similar to the Bucs'. He urged them to be patient, then concluded by predicting it would take at least two to three more years for the team to be competitive.

In the back of the room, an elderly man got to his feet and shouted, "Some of us don't have that long!"

• • •

The Hannahs are brothers three—John, with the New England Patriots; Charles, with the Tampa Bay Buccaneers; and David, who was a collegian at Alabama when he was asked whether he and his brothers had tempers. "We all used to have pretty good tempers," David acknowledged. "We'd go at each other pretty good sometimes."

But he denied a story making the rounds that the three of them fought with two-by-fours. "That's just not so," said David. "It was with baseball bats. We'd never hit each other with a two-by-four."

• • •

Howard Cosell may not have too many fans, but he has at least one who acknowledges he knew Howard as a youngster—when he was just as loud and contentious as he is now.

Ira Topping knew Cosell when he was little Howard Cohen playing touch football in Brooklyn, New York. Little Howard always seemed to be on the winning team. "He'd win most of the games by arguing," Topping revealed. "We'd spend half the time playing and half the time arguing and Howard

was the biggest mouth of them all."

• • •

The Oakland Raiders had just stepped off the plane when coach John Madden was asked how the flight was.

"Fine," said Madden. "We saw a movie, *Jaws*. It was just great. Boy, I wish I had that thing at linebacker."

• • •

Don Meredith, now a TV analyst but once the quarterback for Tom Landry's Dallas Cowboys, remembers one game in which he had particular difficulty calling a play after he had decided the one sent in from the sidelines wouldn't work.

Meredith immediately called an audible, and the opposition middle linebacker moved in position to foil the play. So Meredith called still another audible, only to look up and see the linebacker again switching to where the play would be run.

Thoroughly frustrated, Meredith leaned toward the line of scrimmage and yelled at the linebacker, "Why don't you stay where Tom Landry said you'd be?"

• • •

Ezra Johnson, a defensive end for the Green Bay Packers, had been fined $1,000 for eating a hot dog on the sidelines while the game was going on. He thought the fine was too severe considering the nature of the crime.

"I was just hungry," he explained. "I didn't wave it around or anything."

• • •

It was cold the day the Cincinnati Bengals and Cleveland Browns met in the final game of the season. The Bengals had won, and now reporters were pestering Browns' coach Sam Rutigliano.

Specifically, they wanted to know if the falling temperatures had been a major factor in the number of turnovers committed by the Browns.

"I checked everybody before the game," Rutigliano snapped, "and they were all ninety-eight point six."

• • •

The Dallas Cowboys were leading the Pittsburgh Steelers 10–7 early in the fourth quarter of Super Bowl X, with the ball in the Cowboys' possession on their own 10-yard line. In the Cowboys' huddle, quarterback Roger Staubach began to call the next play, then noticed someone who obviously didn't belong.

"I looked around," said Staubach, "and there, standing between all these sweating giants, was a girl. I didn't know who she was, or where she came from."

Later investigation revealed her name was Bambi Brown. She was an exotic dancer from Atlanta who had sprinted out of the stands to the Dallas huddle in a white pants suit trimmed with blue and red.

Bambi Brown remained in the Dallas huddle long enough to hand tackle Rayfield Wright a good-luck charm, then was steered off the field by police. "It was a horseshoe on a chain," Wright said. "I don't believe in those things. After the police took her away, I just threw it away."

Not a good move, Rayfield. Everything seemed to go wrong for the Cowboys after that. They were unable to move the ball for three downs, had their punt blocked for a safety, and on the next series the Steelers took a 12–10 lead they never relinquished en route to a 21–17 victory.

What do you think Rayfield?

"Maybe," he answered, "I should have hung onto it. But I'm not superstitious. I don't think the team thought about it after that. I know I didn't. I was too busy trying to work on my concentration. Execution is what is going to make you win. How can a good-luck charm help you win?"

• • •

Asked if defensive tackle Joe Greene of the Pittsburgh Steelers was the toughest he ever played against, running back Marv Hubbard of the Oakland Raiders said, "Joe Greene comes off the line so fast sometimes you don't even have time to close your eyes."

• • •

Eddie LeBaron always will remain something of a unique figure in NFL history because he stood only 5 feet 7 inches tall, rather short for a quarterback.

While he was with the Redskins, he attended a father-and-son night for parishioners of a Washington church, at which he was the guest of honor. As such, he was seated on the dais, where he sat quietly while dinner was served.

There was considerable scurrying around by the waitresses as they put plates down on the table, but no one put anything in front of LeBaron until a lady with a distinct brogue did. And, as she did, she said, "Don't ye be leavin' anything, sonny."

At that, LeBaron looked down at the plate—and blinked in amazement. She had given him a children's portion.

• • •

John Breen, former general manager of the Houston Oilers, was asked about some of the problems the club had in the early days of the American Football League. He pointed to one particularly difficult period when the Oilers had trouble moving the ball.

"We were tipping off our plays." he explained. "Whenever we broke from the huddle, three backs were laughing and one was pale as a ghost."

• • •

For more years than anyone cared to remember, Art Donovan, the Hall of Fame defensive tackle for the Baltimore Colts, wore a red sport coat. Finally, several teammates suggested the coat should be retired. But Donovan insisted on wearing it to the West Coast on the club's final road trip of the season.

As soon as the team entered the lobby of its hotel, Dick Szymanski went over to Donovan, reached out for the coat, and tore the middle seam apart, leaving Donovan standing with the first two-piece jacket in the history of men's apparel. Donovan got the message and decided it was time the jacket was discarded. He took off what was left of it, trampled it under his feet, and then draped it over the statue of a Greek god standing naked in the lobby.

As soon as Donovan had his back turned, equipment manager Fred Schubach retrieved the jacket and had it repaired, then put it in Donovan's room. When Donovan returned in the evening, there it was. So he gave it to a maid with explicit instructions to have it discarded.

However, wherever Donovan went during the trip, the coat seemed sure to follow. When he left the hotel, a bellhop ran up and said he didn't want Donovan to leave it behind. Donovan took it with him, but threw it out of a bus window. During dinner in a fashionable restaurant, Donovan was paged and handed a package. Inside, was the jacket.

Donovan took it back to the hotel with him, pulled out a five-dollar bill, and told the desk man to have the jacket burned. That seemed to work; for the remainder of the road trip he was free of the coat.

The Colts returned to Baltimore at Christmas. When Donovan got home, his wife wished him a Merry Christmas and gave him a package she insisted was something special. Donovan immediately proceeded to open it—and saw red.

• • •

Linebacker Warren Capone of the Dallas Cowboys was asked his relationship to gangster Al Capone.

"I'm Italian, but I never knew the gentleman," he said. "I'm not crazy about claiming him. He never left me any money."

• • •

In his short NFL career, coach John McKay of the Tampa Bay Buccaneers has gained quite a reputation as a football humorist. It all began during his first seasons with the expansion Bucs as they battled to win their first game.

Near the end of his second season, McKay was looking for a way to end a 24-game winless streak—and decided that he might try to do it by showing up naked for a game with Atlanta.

"Maybe, it'll be lucky," he explained. "Maybe, it'll distract the other quarterback. I have tried everything else. I have worn twenty-four different outfits at the twenty-four different games we have lost. I have slept on my right side the night before, the left, stomach, back, slept sitting up, on the floor. I go to church. I study different passages. I sing this song, that song. I eat this or that as a pre-game meal. I don't know."

McKay, however, did not show up sans clothes. And the Bucs lost again. "I'm so embarrassed," he said, "I've taken to wearing a disguise. I've got a fake beard and fake nose, but people keep stopping me on the street asking for my autograph. They think I'm Abraham Lincoln."

• • •

The Zero Club—a secret society formed by three members of the Dallas Cowboys—is on its last two legs. And that's really just as well because Larry Cole has violated all the principles of the club's charter.

The Zero Club was formed in the late 1960s by three young members of the Cowboys—Larry Cole, Blaine Nye, and Pat Toomay—who believed it was the inalienable right of every lineman to play in total obscurity. And, when they weren't playing, the members of the Zero Club reveled in their one activity—doing absolutely nothing. Apathy was their hallmark. According to lore, the Zero Club called meetings all the time, but no one attended.

During the seventies, age began to take its toll on the club. Toomay was traded in 1974, Nye retired in 1976. That left Cole as the Lone Zero. Obviously he couldn't recruit new members—such initiative would violate the club's tenets. In 1980, the Zero Club sank to its all-time low when Cole allowed himself to intercept a pass and run it back 43 yards for the winning touchdown in a 14–10 victory over Washington. Nye and Toomay would have looked on in horror, if they permitted themselves that emotion.

And, not only did Cole score a touchdown, he actually enjoyed it—spiking the ball in the end zone to make the point. "Toomay and Nye will probably never forgive me," a flustered Cole admitted after the game. "I don't know what got into me. I can't remember the last time I had that much attention."

Then, speaking like the last true Zero, he added, "I just wish I had the talent to enjoy it."

• • •

Tom Williams, the Houston Oilers' assistant general manager, who is black, was asked to tick off some of the qualifications of the team's number-one draft choice, tight end Mike Barber, who is white.

"He weighs two hundred twenty pounds, has great hands, runs the forty in four-and-a-half, does the high hurdles in thirteen point seven, and high jumps six-six," said Williams. "Sounds like he was born the wrong color."

• • •

The Pittsburgh Steelers certainly had an amazing impact on the NFL in the 1970s. And so did some of the merchandise marketed in support of the team, particularly the item called the Terrible Towel.

The black-and-gold towel was developed during the 1978 season by Pittsburgh broadcaster Myron Cope for the Steelers' drive to their third Super Bowl victory. And, when the Steelers reached the Super Bowl in Miami, some 20,000 Terrible Towels were sold.

Even coach Don Shula of the Miami Dolphins—a spectator at Super Bowl XIII in the Orange Bowl—felt the impact of Cope's brainchild. "I sat in the stands with my kids," Shula said. "I ended up paying thirty-five bucks or something for seven Terrible Towels."

Eye-to-eye and shoulder-to-shoulder is the intimacy that football engenders. Whether it is work or play is a personal question, answerable sometimes only by the man who safely holds the ball.

All photographs included in this book were
taken by the photographers of FOCUS ON SPORTS,
222 East 46th Street, New York, New York 10017,
with the exception of the following by
UNITED PRESS INTERNATIONAL: 12, 38–39, 41,
46, 57, 64–65, 72–73.